SCIENCE
(AQA)

Interactive Revision Tutor

Nigel Saunders

Published by BBC Active, an imprint of Educational Publishers LLP, part of the Pearson Education Group, Edinburgh Gate, Harlow, Essex CM20 2JE, England

ISBN: 978-1-4066-4460-9

Printed and bound in China CTPSC/01

The Publisher's policy is to use paper manufactured from sustainable forests.

First published 2008

Cover photograph: Alamy

System requirements
PC: Windows® IBM compatible PC, Intel Pentium 3 600 MHz processor or equivalent, 256 MB RAM, 1GB RAM for Windows Vista®, 1GB free space (or 10% of drive capacity, whichever is higher), sound card, CD-ROM 16x drive, 1024 x 768 screen resolution at 16 bits per pixel (1000s of colours)
MAC: G4 processor at 700 MHz or faster, 256 MB RAM, 1GB free space (or 10% of drive capacity, whichever is higher) Microsoft Internet Explorer® 6.1 SP2 or Macintosh Safari™ 1.3, Adobe Flash® Player 8 or higher, Adobe Reader® 7 or higher Headphones recommended

CW00375783

Contents

Physics

How to use Bitesize Interactive Revision Tutor

Begin with the CD-ROM. There are **six easy steps** to using the CD-ROM – and to creating your own personal revision programme. Follow these steps and you'll be fully prepared for the exam without wasting time on areas you already know.

Step 1: Check
The Topic checker will help you figure out what you know – and what you need to revise.

Step 2: Plan
When you know which topics you need to revise, enter them into the handy Revision planner. You'll get a daily reminder to make sure you're on track.

Step 3: Revise
From the Topic checker, you can go straight to the topic pages that contain all the facts you need to know.

- Give yourself the edge with the ReviseBite buttons. These link directly to the relevant section on the BBC *Bitesize Revision* website.

- AudioBite buttons let you listen to more about the topic to boost your knowledge even further.

Step 4: Practise
Check your understanding by answering the Practice questions. Click on each question to see the correct answer.

Step 5: Test
TestBite buttons link directly to a test on the topic on the BBC *Bitesize Revision* website.

Step 6: Exam
Are you ready for the exam? ExamQ buttons take you to an exam question on the topics you've just revised.

You can choose to go through every topic from beginning to end by clicking on the Interactive book and selecting topics on the Contents page.

 The Last-minute learner gives you the most important facts in a few pages for that final revision session.

 Find all of the Exam questions in one place by clicking on the Exam questions tab.

 You can access the information on these pages at any time from the link on the Topic checker or by clicking on the Help tab. You can also do the Tutorial which provides step-by-step instructions on how to use the CD-ROM and gives you an overview of all the features available. You can find the Tutorial on the launch screen when you first insert the CD-ROM.

Other features include:

 Click on these arrows to switch the buttons to the opposite side of the screen.

 Click on Page turn to stop the pages turning over like a book.

 Click on Hide web links if you're working offline.

 Click on this arrow to go back to the previous screen.

 Click on the Single page icon to see a single page.

 Click on these arrows to go backward or forward one page at a time.

 Click on these arrows to go to the beginning or the end of the section you are in.

Click on any section of the text on a topic page to zoom in for a closer look.

N.B. You may come across some exercises that you can't do on-screen, such as circling or underlining, in these cases you should use the printed book.

Introduction continued

About this book

This book is your complete revision companion for AQA GCSE Science. It gives you the three things you need for successful revision:

1. Each topic is organised clearly and explained on one spread.
2. The most important ideas in each topic are highlighted so you can find them quickly.
3. There are lots of practice questions at the end of each topic and at the back of the book.

Each topic is organised in the same way:

- **The bare bones**

    This is a summary of the main ideas, an introduction to the topic, and a good starting point to check what you already know.

- **Key facts**

    The most important ideas are highlighted in yellow boxes in each topic.

- **Exam tips**

    These are highlighted in blue boxes. They give advice on common mistakes and good answers.

- **Practice questions**

    A range of short-answer questions at the end of each topic.

The extra sections at the back of the book will help you check your progress. They will help you to be confident about your knowledge and understanding of science.

Exam questions

- Multiple choice questions similar to the ones you will meet in AQA's GCSE Science module examinations, with answers. They are suitable for Foundation Tier and Higher Tier candidates.

Topic checkers

- Quick questions for each topic.
- As you revise a set of topics, have a go at answering these questions. Put ticks or crosses next to them so you can see how you are improving.
- The next time you revise the same topics, have a go at the questions again. Do this until you have a column of ticks.

Complete the facts

- Another resource to help you revise. Fill in the gaps to complete the facts, then check your answers at the end of the section.

Last-minute learner

- A series of pages with the most important ideas condensed to one page per unit.

The examiners are not trying to trick you. They just want to give you the chance to show what you can do. But they are not mind readers. They can only mark what you actually do on the examination paper. Here are some general tips:

- Read through the whole paper for a few minutes at the start and tick the easiest questions as you go.
- Answer your ticked questions first. This will help you feel more calm and confident.
- Tackle the remaining questions.
- Remember to read the questions carefully and underline important words. The information at the start is there to help you, so don't ignore it.

More advice for written exams

Keeping to time
- The written exams work out at one mark per minute on average. You are likely to run out of time if you spend ten minutes on a question worth just one mark.
- The amount of space and the number of marks available are clues to how much to write. You probably won't have written enough if you write one line when there are four marks and six lines.

Calculations
- Write down the equation you need to answer the question.
- Show your working out.
- Show the units if asked.
- Check that the answer makes sense.
  For example, is a snail really likely to move at 100 m/s on its own?

Graphs
- Use a sharp pencil.
- You are likely be given a partly completed graph to finish in the Foundation Tier exam.
  In the Higher Tier exam you are likely to have to draw your own axes. Try to use more than half the area of the graph paper without choosing a strange scale.
- Label both axes and include the units.
- Plot each point with a neat cross, or use a ruler to draw bars.
- In a bar chart, don't waste time shading in the bars unless the question asks you to. In a line graph, draw a line or smooth curve with a single stroke of your pencil.

The nervous system

THE BARE BONES

➤ Receptors detect changes in the environment called stimuli.
➤ Information from receptors travels along neurones to the brain.
➤ The brain coordinates the response.
➤ Reflex actions are fast and automatic.

A Receptors and stimuli

1 A **stimulus** is a change in the surroundings. Stimuli include sound, light, chemicals, touch, pain, pressure, temperature and changes in position.

KEY FACT **2** A **receptor** is *a cell or group of cells* that can detect a stimulus. For example, receptors in the ear detect sound, receptors in the eye detect light, and receptors in the tongue detect chemicals in food and drink.

> Ears, eyes and the tongue are sense organs. You don't need to know about their structure or function for the exams.
>
> **Exam tip**

B Neurones and the brain

1 Nerve cells are called **neurones**. They carry information from one place to another in the body as electrical signals.

KEY FACT **2** Information travels as electrical impulses along nerve cells from the receptors to the brain.

3 The brain coordinates the response to the stimulus. The response involves effectors and other nerve cells.

C Synapses

KEY FACT **1** A synapse is the gap between two nerve cells.

2 Electrical impulses cannot cross the synapse. Instead, chemicals called *neurotransmitters* diffuse across it. They are produced by one of the nerve cells, and make the other nerve cell send information.

nerve impulse passes along axon of a sensory neurone

synapse

nerve impulse passes along axon of motor neurone

the nerve ending releases a chemical which diffuses across the synapse

D Reflex actions

KEY FACT **1** Reflex actions are fast and automatic. They do not need to be learned and they happen without us thinking about them. They involve receptors, different types of nerve cell, and effectors.

2 Sensory neurones carry information from receptors.

Relay neurones in the spinal cord carry information from sensory neurones to motor neurones.

Motor neurones carry information to effectors.

Effectors are muscles and glands.

KEY FACT **3** The sequence of events is:

stimulus
↓
receptor
↓
sensory neurone
↓
relay neurone
↓
motor neurone
↓
effector

receptor detects a stimulus e.g. touch

impulse travels to central nervous system (CNS)

sensory neurone

a relay neurone connects sensory and motor neurones in the CNS

connecting or **relay** neurone

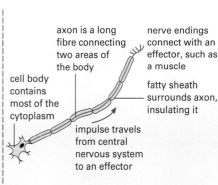

cell body contains most of the cytoplasm

axon is a long fibre connecting two areas of the body

nerve endings connect with an effector, such as a muscle

fatty sheath surrounds axon, insulating it

impulse travels from central nervous system to an effector

motor neurone

PRACTICE QUESTIONS

1 What is a synapse?

2 You rapidly pull your hand away if you accidentally touch something hot.

Outline the sequence of events in this reflex action.

THE BARE BONES

> ➤ The body's internal conditions are controlled.
> ➤ The nervous system and hormones are involved in this control.
> ➤ Hormones are chemicals secreted by glands.
> ➤ The bloodstream transports hormones to their target organs.

A Some conditions to control

1 The body's cells and the chemicals they contain are damaged if the conditions change too much.

KEY FACT ➤ **2** The internal conditions that must be controlled within tight limits include:

- water content (the different chemicals in the body must not be too dilute or too concentrated)
- ion content (such as sodium ions from the *salt* in our food)
- blood sugar level (to provide cells with a constant source of *energy*)
- temperature (*enzymes* work best at a certain temperature).

B Controlling water and ion content

1 *Water* leaves the body from the *lungs* when we breathe out.

2 *Water and ions* leave the body from the *skin* when we sweat and from the *kidneys* in urine.

C Sports drinks

1 The manufacturers of sports drinks claim that their products are better than ordinary drinks when people take exercise. Sports drinks contain dissolved ions and sugars. The aim is to replace the water, ions and sugars lost from the body during exercise.

Exam tip

You may be given information in a table or graph about sports drinks to evaluate in the exam.

D Hortmones

KEY FACT

1 Hormones are *chemicals* produced or secreted by glands. They are transported in the *bloodstream* to their *target organs*, where they cause a response or change.

2 Many processes in the body are coordinated by hormones. For example:

- ADH controls the amount of urine produced by the kidneys
- insulin makes the liver convert glucose to glycogen
- adrenaline makes the heart beat faster
- sex hormones control puberty and reproduction.

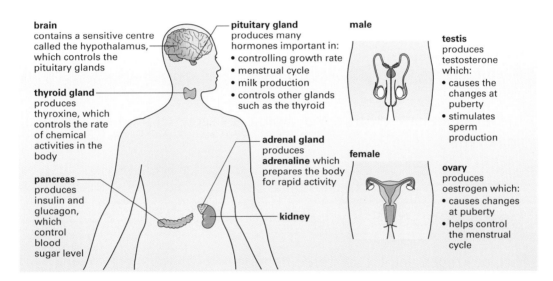

brain
contains a sensitive centre called the hypothalamus, which controls the pituitary glands

thyroid gland
produces thyroxine, which controls the rate of chemical activities in the body

pancreas
produces insulin and glucagon, which control blood sugar level

pituitary gland
produces many hormones important in:
- controlling growth rate
- menstrual cycle
- milk production
- controls other glands such as the thyroid

adrenal gland
produces **adrenaline** which prepares the body for rapid activity

kidney

male

testis
produces testosterone which:
- causes the changes at puberty
- stimulates sperm production

female

ovary
produces oestrogen which:
- causes changes at puberty
- helps control the menstrual cycle

E Nervous system and hormonal system compared

nervous system	hormonal system
information travels very quickly	hormones are transported more slowly
response is short-lived	response is often long-lasting
usually act on a small area	often have widespread effects

PRACTICE QUESTIONS

1 Name two internal conditions that must be controlled by the body.

2 How are hormones transported in the body?

3 Suggest an advantage of being able to coordinate life processes by two systems, one involving nerves and the other involving hormones.

THE BARE BONES

➤ The menstrual cycle is controlled by several hormones.

➤ Hormones can be used to control fertility in women.

A The menstrual cycle

1 Having a period is called menstruation. A woman's monthly cycle is called the menstrual cycle. It lasts about 28 days.

KEY FACTS

2 During the menstrual cycle, an egg is released from an ovary and there are changes in the thickness of the lining of the womb.

3 These changes are controlled by hormones secreted by the pituitary gland and ovaries.

B FSH, oestrogen and LH

1 FSH, oestrogen and LH are three hormones involved in controlling the *menstrual cycle*.

KEY FACTS

2 FSH is secreted by the pituitary gland:

• it causes an egg to mature in an ovary

• it stimulates the ovaries to release oestrogen.

3 Oestrogen is secreted by the ovaries:

• it stops FSH being produced (so that only one egg matures in a cycle)

• it stimulates the pituitary gland to release LH

• it causes the lining of the womb to thicken.

4 LH is secreted by the pituitary gland. It causes an egg to be released at around day 14.

Progesterone is a hormone that maintains the lining of the womb if the egg is fertilised.

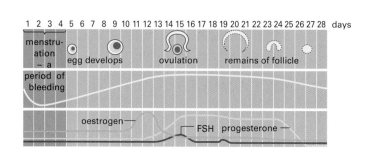

C Oral contraceptives

KEY FACT 1 Oral contraceptives prevent women becoming pregnant. They contain hormones that prevent FSH being produced. This means that eggs do not mature in the ovaries.

2 Oral contraceptives allow couples to choose when to start a family.

3 Oral contraceptives cause problems for some women, including weight gain and mood swings.

D Fertility drugs

KEY FACT 1 One reason why a woman might be infertile is that her level of FSH is too low to cause eggs to mature. Fertility drugs containing FSH increase the chance of a woman becoming pregnant. They boost the level of FSH and cause eggs to mature.

2 Fertility drugs increase the chances of couples starting a family if they are having difficulty doing so.

E IVF

1 IVF stands for *in vitro fertilisation*. It involves fertilising a woman's egg outside her body in the laboratory. The embryo is allowed to develop for a short time and then implanted into the woman's womb.

2 IVF can help infertile couples have a family. The embryo can be tested for genetic disorders. But some people worry that couples may want 'designer babies'. For example, they may want to have a boy rather than a girl, or an embryo with a particular feature, such as high intelligence.

PRACTICE QUESTIONS

1 Where is FSH secreted from, and what does it do?
2 Where is oestrogen secreted from, and what does it do?
3 Explain how FSH and oestrogen may be used to control fertility in women.

Diet and exercise

THE BARE BONES

- ➤ A person can become too thin or too fat if their diet is unbalanced.
- ➤ Some people in the developing world suffer illness owing to lack of food.
- ➤ Some people in the developed world suffer illness owing to too much food and too little exercise.

A   A balanced diet

KEY FACT **1** A balanced diet contains the correct nutrients in the right amounts. It supplies the right amount of energy for the amount of activity a person does.

nutrient	why we need it	typical source
carbohydrate	energy	potatoes, rice
protein	growth and repair	eggs, meat
fat	energy	butter, vegetable oils
vitamins	maintaining health	fruit, vegetables, bread
minerals	maintaining health	meat, vegetables

The main nutrients, why they are needed, and some typical sources of them.
Fibre and water are also needed in the diet.

2 Malnutrition happens if a diet is not balanced.
The effects of malnourishment include:

- becoming too thin or too fat
- deficiency diseases if the amount of a nutrient in the diet is too low
- diseases linked to excess weight if the amount of energy supplied by the diet is too high.

B   Deficiency diseases

KEY FACT **1** Some people in the developing world can suffer from a lack of sufficient food. They suffer health problems, including *irregular periods* in women and a *reduced resistance* to infection.

C Exercise and diet

EY FACT **1** The rate at which the various chemical reactions take place in your body's cells is called the metabolic rate. It is affected by various factors, including:

- the *amount of muscle* you have compared to your *body fat*
- the *amount of activity* you do
- *inherited factors.*

2 Exercise *increases* the metabolic rate, and it stays higher for some time after the exercise is over.

D Excess weight

EY FACT **1** *Less food is needed* when the surroundings are *warm*, and when a person is taking *little exercise*. For example, someone sitting at a chair in an office needs less energy from their food than someone working outside in a physically demanding job.

2 If someone eats too much food, and takes too little exercise, they become *overweight*. Very overweight people are described as *obese*. High levels of obesity are a problem in the developed world.

EY FACT **3** Diseases linked to excess weight include:

- diabetes (high levels of sugar in the blood)
- heart disease
- arthritis (worn and swollen joints)
- high blood pressure.

PRACTICE QUESTIONS

1 What is a balanced diet?

2 Outline some problems associated with too little food in the diet.

3 Outline some problems associated with too much food in the diet.

Cholesterol and salt

THE BARE BONES

➤ High levels of cholesterol in the blood increase the risk of heart disease.

➤ LDLs are 'bad' cholesterol and HDLs are 'good' cholesterol.

➤ Unsaturated fats in the diet help to improve the balance between LDLs and HDLs.

➤ Excess salt in the diet can cause high blood pressure.

A Cholesterol

KEY FACTS

1 Cholesterol is a substance found in the blood. It is made by the *liver* from saturated fats in the diet.

2 The amount of cholesterol produced by the liver depends upon *inherited factors* and *diet*:

• Saturated fats increase blood cholesterol levels.

• Unsaturated fats help to decrease blood cholesterol levels.

3 *High levels* of cholesterol in the blood increase the chance of developing cardiovascular disease – *heart disease* and *blocked arteries*.

Arteries have thick, muscular, elastic walls. Fatty deposits can narrow arteries and may block them.

B LDLs and HDLs

1 Cholesterol is transported around the body in the bloodstream attached to proteins. The combination of cholesterol and protein is called lipoprotein.

KEY FACTS **2** There are *two types of lipoprotein*:

• low-density lipoprotein or LDL   • high-density lipoprotein or HDL.

3 LDLs carry cholesterol *from the liver* to the cells of the body. They are sometimes called *'bad' cholesterol*.

4 HDLs carry excess cholesterol from the cells back *to the liver*. They are sometimes called *'good' cholesterol*.

KEY FACT

1. About 30% of blood cholesterol is carried as HDLs. The balance of LDL to HDL is important for health:

   - Higher proportions of LDLs increase the risk of cardiovascular disease.
   - Higher proportions of HDLs reduce the risk cardiovascular disease.

2. Saturated fats increase blood cholesterol levels. Foods such as meat and eggs are rich in saturated fats.

3. Mono-unsaturated fats and polyunsaturated fats may help to reduce cholesterol levels in the blood, and improve the balance of LDL to HDL. Foods such as olive oil and oily fish are rich in unsaturated fats.

> Statins are a type of medicine that reduces blood cholesterol levels. You may be given information in the exam so you can evaluate the effect of statins on cardiovascular disease.

Exam tip

D Processed foods

KEY FACTS

1. *Processed foods* often contain a lot of *fat*. Too much of these foods in the diet can lead to *obesity* and raised blood cholesterol levels. This in turn increases the risk of cardiovascular disease.

2. Processed foods often also contain a lot of *salt*. Too much salt causes *increased blood pressure* in about 30% of the population.

3. High blood pressure increases the risk of cardiovascular disease.

PRACTICE QUESTIONS

1. Where is cholesterol made in the body?
2. Outline some differences between LDLs and HDLs.
3. Explain how eating too much processed food can lead to ill-health.

Medical drugs

THE BARE BONES

➤ New drugs need to be tested to make sure that they are safe and effective.

➤ Thalidomide is a drug that caused abnormal arm and leg development in unborn babies. It was banned, but is now used successfully to treat leprosy.

A Medical drugs

KEY FACTS

1 Drugs are substances that change chemical processes in the body. These changes can be helpful or harmful, depending on the drug.

2 Many drugs are found naturally. Such drugs have been known about for many years.

3 For example, the ancient Greeks used willow bark to help cure fevers and pains. Salicylic acid is the active ingredient in willow bark. It has a similar chemical structure to aspirin. Natural substances are a source of raw materials for developing new drugs.

salicyclic acid   aspirin

B Testing drugs

KEY FACT

1 Scientists are developing new drugs and these must be *tested*. It is important that new drugs are *effective* (they actually work) and are *safe* (they will not cause dangerous side effects).

2 There are three main stages in testing new drugs:

- Using computer models and human cells grown in the *laboratory*. Many substances fail this test because they are *toxic* and damage cells.

- New drugs passing the first stage are tested on *animals*. A known amount is given to the animals, which are then monitored carefully for any side-effects.

- Drugs that have passed the second stage are used in *clinical trials*. They are trialled on healthy volunteers to discover any side effects. They are then tested on people with the illness to ensure they work.

Remember

It is a legal requirement in the UK that all new drugs are tested on animals before reaching the human trial stage. But it is illegal to test cosmetics and tobacco products on animals.

C Thalidomide

1 *Thalidomide* is a drug that was originally developed as a sleeping tablet in the 1950s.

2 It was also found to be effective at reducing the symptoms of morning sickness in *pregnant women*. But it had not been tested for this different use. Between the late 1950s and early 1960s thousands of babies were born with deformities, such as abnormally short arms or legs.

3 Thalidomide was banned because of its effects on unborn babies. It has been licensed recently to treat *leprosy*, a disease of the skin and nerves caused by a bacterium.

Remember

The thalidomide story shows what can happen if drugs are not tested sufficiently before use. Its effectiveness against morning sickness and leprosy were discovered by accident.

PRACTICE QUESTIONS

1 What is a drug?

2 Describe the main stages in testing a new medical drug.

3 Explain why female leprosy sufferers cannot be prescribed thalidomide if they are pregnant or not using contraceptives.

Recreational drugs

THE BARE BONES

➤ Some people use recreational drugs to alter their mood. Drugs can be legal or illegal.

➤ People may become addicted to a drug and experience withdrawal symptoms if they stop taking it.

➤ Tobacco and alcohol are legal recreational drugs. They can damage the body.

A Tobacco

1 Tobacco smoke contains around 4000 different chemicals. Many of these are harmful.

KEY FACTS **2** Nicotine is the *addictive* substance in tobacco smoke. It creates a powerful dependency so that smokers quickly become addicted. Smokers have unpleasant *withdrawal symptoms* if they try to give up smoking.

3 Tobacco smoke contains *carbon monoxide*. This *reduces the ability of the blood to carry oxygen* because it combines with haemoglobin in red blood cells. Smoking during pregnancy is very dangerous. It reduces the amount of oxygen available to the growing fetus. This can cause babies to have a *low weight*. It can also cause miscarriage and premature birth.

Carbon monoxide reduces the oxygen-carrying capacity of the red blood cells.

4 The effects of carbon monoxide put extra strain on the circulatory system, and cause an increased risk of cardiovascular disease and strokes.

KEY FACT **5** Tobacco smoke also contains *carcinogens*, such as *tar*. These are substances that cause *cancer*. Smoking increases the risk of lung cancer, mouth cancer and throat cancer.

You may be given information to evaluate in the exam about smoking and health. Use this with your knowledge and understanding of science to answer the question.

Exam tip

B Alcohol

1 **Ethanol** is the alcohol found in alcoholic drinks such as beer, wine and spirits. It is usually just called *alcohol*.

2 Alcohol affects the *nervous system*. It *slows down reactions* and helps people to relax.

3 Too much alcohol leads to a *lack of self-control*. Drinkers may not realise how much they are drinking. They may become *unconscious*, and may even fall into a *coma*. Alcohol damages the *liver* and *brain* in the longer term.

C Legal and illegal drugs

1 Alcohol and tobacco are legal recreational drugs.

2 *Illegal drugs* include substances that are banned by law, and prescription drugs that have been modified. Heroin and cocaine are illegal recreational drugs. They are very addictive, and may cause permanent mental problems.

3 More people use legal recreational drugs than use illegal drugs. So the overall impact on health is greater from legal than illegal drugs.

4 Drugs change chemical processes in the body, so they all have the potential to damage health. Addictive recreational drugs may damage health indirectly. For example:

  • users may turn to crime to pay for their drugs, which affects the lives of other people

  • used needles can transmit diseases such as AIDS and hepatitis from infected blood.

PRACTICE QUESTIONS

1 What does 'addicted' mean?

2 Explain the problems caused by nicotine, carbon monoxide and tar in tobacco smoke.

3 Which parts of the body are affected by alcohol?

4 Suggest why smokers may be reluctant to give up smoking, even though the link between smoking and increased risk of lung cancer has been firmly established.

Pathogens and disease

THE BARE BONES

➤ Pathogens are microorganisms which cause infectious diseases.

➤ Bacteria and viruses are pathogens. They reproduce rapidly inside the body and release toxins that make us feel ill.

➤ White blood cells ingest pathogens, produce antitoxins, and produce antibodies that destroy particular pathogens.

A Pathogens

KEY FACT **1** Pathogens are microorganisms that cause infectious diseases. Bacteria and viruses are pathogens.

2 Bacteria are tiny living cells – the largest are only 10 micrometres long (10 µm or 10 thousandths of a millimetre).

Diseases caused by bacteria include food poisoning, cholera, typhoid and whooping cough.

KEY FACT **3** Bacteria can *multiply rapidly* once inside the body. They release poisons or toxins that make us feel ill.

4 Viruses are even smaller than bacteria. They consist of a fragment of genetic material inside a protective protein coat.

KEY FACT **5** Viruses can only reproduce inside host cells, and they damage the cell when they do this.

6 Once a virus gets inside a cell, it *multiplies rapidly*. Viruses eventually fill the whole cell, bursting it open and letting the viruses escape.

Diseases caused by viruses include colds, influenza (flu), measles, mumps, rubella, tetanus, chicken pox and AIDS.

EY FACT **1** White blood cells help to defend the body against pathogens:

- They produce **antitoxins**. These are chemicals that counteract the *toxins* produced by pathogens.

- They *ingest* pathogens.

Remember

White blood cells do not *eat* pathogens. They surround them, engulfing them and destroying them with reactive chemicals.

2 Some of the substances in pathogens and on their surfaces are recognised by the body as foreign. These substances are called **antigens**. Different pathogens have different antigens.

EY FACT **3** White blood cells can produce proteins called **antibodies**. These can attach to antigens. Different antibodies recognise different antigens. Chemical signals are released when antibodies attach to a pathogen. Two things can happen as a result:

- chemicals are released that *destroy the pathogen*

- white blood cells are attracted and *ingest the pathogen*.

1. white blood cells make antibodies

2. antibodies match antigen

3. lock together

4. white blood cell engulfs antigen and destroys it

⊔ antibody

▯ antigen on a bacterium

Make sure you show you understand that the pathogens are not the disease. Instead, they are the **cause** of the disease.

Exam tip

PRACTICE QUESTIONS

1 What is a pathogen?

2 How do pathogens make us feel ill?

3 Outline three ways in which white blood cells can help to defend the body against pathogens.

THE BARE BONES

➤ Antibiotics kill bacteria but not viruses.
➤ It is difficult to develop drugs that kill viruses without damaging the body.
➤ Many strains of bacteria have developed resistance to antibiotics because of natural selection.

A Relieving symptoms

KEY FACT **1** Some medicines *relieve the symptoms* of a disease without actually killing the pathogens.

2 *Painkillers* are like this. They reduce the feeling of pain, but do not kill the pathogens or repair the damage caused by the pathogens.

B Antibiotics

1 *Penicillin* was the first antibiotic discovered.

KEY FACTS **2** Antibiotics are chemicals that *kill bacteria* inside the body.
They help to cure diseases caused by bacteria.

3 Antibiotics cannot kill viruses. Viruses reproduce inside the body's cells. It is difficult to develop drugs that kill viruses without also damaging the body's cells.

4 Antibiotics are produced naturally by certain fungi, but modern antibiotics are designed by scientists and manufactured.

antibiotic	how it works
Penicillin	breaks down cell walls
Erythromycin Vancomycin	stops protein synthesis
Ciprofloxacin	stops DNA replication

Four different antibiotics and how they work.

C Antibiotic-resistant bacteria

1 Many strains of bacteria have developed *resistance* to one or more antibiotics. This means that the antibiotics have no effect on them.

2 *MRSA*, or 'methicillin-resistant *Staphylococcus aureus*', is a strain of bacteria that is resistant to antibiotics based on penicillin. It is sometimes called a 'superbug' because of this.

3 Bacteria develop antibiotic resistance because of *natural selection*.

4 In any population of bacteria, some bacteria may naturally be resistant to an antibiotic. When a patient is given this antibiotic, the bacteria are all killed, except for the resistant ones. These are able to reproduce and pass on their resistance to later generations of bacteria.

D Treating infections

1 Ignaz Semmelweis was a hospital doctor in the 19th century. He realised the importance of cleanliness in hospitals. He insisted on keeping the hospital clean and on personal hygiene amongst the staff. This reduced the risk of infection. But his ideas were ignored at the time, because no-one knew that infectious diseases were caused by pathogens that could be killed.

2 When antibiotics were discovered, they were relied upon too much to treat disease and prevent infections. In the recent past, hospitals were not always clean enough to reduce the risk of infection. Nowadays great care is taken to maintain hygiene.

3 It is important to *avoid over-use of antibiotics*. This reduces the chance of new antibiotic-resistant strains developing.

PRACTICE QUESTIONS

1 What is an antibiotic?

2 Explain why colds cannot be cured by antibiotics.

3 Explain why it is important not to use antibiotics when they are not really needed.

THE BARE BONES

➤ People can be immunised against a particular pathogen by vaccination.
➤ A vaccine is a small amount of a dead or inactive form of a pathogen.
➤ A vaccine stimulates white blood cells to make antibodies against the pathogen. This makes the person immune to the pathogen.

A Immunity

1 When someone is infected by a particular pathogen, white blood cells are made that can recognise and destroy that pathogen.

2 After the pathogen has been destroyed, some of these white blood cells remain. If the person is reinfected by the same pathogen, the white blood cells reproduce rapidly. They produce a lot of antibodies against the pathogen very quickly. In this way, people can become immune to a particular pathogen.

3 Vaccination allows people to become immune to a particular pathogen without being infected first.

B Vaccination

KEY FACTS **1** A vaccine consists of small amounts of:
- the *dead pathogen*, or
- *inactive forms* of the pathogen, or
- *antigens* or *toxins* extracted from the pathogen.

2 The vaccine is put into the body, usually by *injection*. It stimulates the production of white blood cells that can make *antibodies* against a particular pathogen.

3 Some of these white blood cells remain in the body after the vaccine has been destroyed by the body.

KEY FACT > **4** If the pathogen enters the body in the future, these white blood cells reproduce rapidly. They produce *a lot of antibodies* against the pathogen *very quickly*. In this way, the person is *immune* to the pathogen without having been infected first.

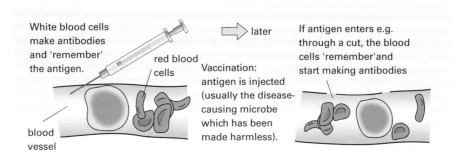

White blood cells make antibodies and 'remember' the antigen.

red blood cells

blood vessel

later

Vaccination: antigen is injected (usually the disease-causing microbe which has been made harmless).

If antigen enters e.g. through a cut, the blood cells 'remember' and start making antibodies

Exam tip

Take care in the exam: it is easy to write that a vaccine is a dead or inactive form of the disease. Instead, you should write that a vaccine is a dead or inactive form of the pathogen.

C   Some vaccines

KEY FACT > **1** Different vaccines are needed to give protection against different diseases. The *MMR* vaccination is given to children. It is a mixture of vaccines that protects them against *measles*, *mumps* and *rubella* (German measles).

2 Vaccines against diphtheria, tetanus, pertussis (whooping cough) and polio are also commonly given.

KEY FACT > **3** Pathogens can change or *mutate* in such a way that a vaccine may no longer be effective. This is particularly true of the influenza (flu) virus. Slightly different vaccines are needed each year.

PRACTICE QUESTIONS

1 What is a vaccine?

2 Explain how vaccination works.

3 Elderly people are particularly at risk from the symptoms of flu.
   Suggest why it is recommended that they receive a flu vaccination every autumn.

Adaptation

THE BARE BONES

➤ Plants compete for light, water, nutrients and space.

➤ Animals compete for food, water, mates and territory.

➤ Organisms have adaptations that allow them to survive in their environment.

A Competition

1 The place where an organism such as an animal or plant lives is called its habitat. The conditions surrounding the organism are the environment.

KEY FACT **2** Organisms need to have a *supply of materials* from their surroundings to survive. They may also need materials from *other organisms*. For example, animals and plants need water, and animals must eat plants or other animals.

3 Organisms can only survive if they can get enough resources. A given habitat may only have a *limited amount* of a particular resource. Organisms must then *compete* with other organisms for this resource. If they are unsuccessful and cannot move to another habitat, they will die.

KEY FACTS **4** Plants may compete with each other for:

- light
- water
- space
- nutrients from the soil, such as mineral salts.

5 Animals may compete with each other for:

- food
- water
- mates
- territory (space in which to live and breed).

Remember

Plants make their own food by *photosynthesis*, so they do not compete for food.

You may be given information about a particular habitat and be asked to suggest the factors that organisms are competing for there.

Exam tip

KEY FACTS

1 Organisms have adaptations or particular features that allow them to survive in their environment.

2 Predators may be warned or put off by adaptations such as *warning colours*, *thorns* or *poisons*. For example, wasps have black and yellow warning stripes and a sting.

3 Animals and plants are adapted in different ways for living in cold or hot environments.

adaptation	Arctic fox	desert rat
body size	large – gives a small surface area compared to its volume, so heat is lost more slowly	small – gives a large surface area compared to its volume, so heat is lost more quickly
insulating layer of fat	thick	thin
insulating layer of fur	thick	thin
camouflage	white	brown

Exam tip

Be prepared to suggest how a particular organism is adapted to its surroundings. You will probably be given information to help.

PRACTICE QUESTIONS

1 State three things that animals may compete for.
2 Explain why grass under a leafy tree does not grow very well.
3 Suggest why the snowshoe hare has white fur in the winter and brown fur in the summer.

Reproduction

THE BARE BONES

> ➤ Chromosomes, found in the nucleus of the cell, carry genes.
> ➤ Different genes control different characteristics of an organism.
> ➤ Sexual reproduction leads to variation in offspring.
> ➤ Asexual reproduction produces clones.

A Genes and chromosomes

1 *DNA* is deoxyribose nucleic acid. It is the chemical that carries *genetic information*. This information is passed from parents to their offspring in DNA.

2 A gene is a section of DNA that carries the code for a particular protein.

KEY FACT **3** Chromosomes are found in the *nucleus of a cell*. They contain many genes. *Different genes* control the development of *different characteristics* in an organism.

> You don't need to know the structure of DNA for your exams.

Exam tip

B Sexual reproduction

1 Sexual reproduction involves two parents.

2 Sex cells are called gametes. In humans:
- *eggs* are the *female* gametes
- *sperm* are the *male* gametes.

KEY FACT **3** In sexual reproduction, male and female gametes *join* to make a new cell. This develops into a new individual. The joining or *fusion* of gametes is called fertilisation.

EY FACT **4** Sexual reproduction leads to *variety in the offspring*. Half the genetic information in the offspring comes from one parent, and half comes from the other parent. So the *genetic information* from two parents is *mixed*. The offspring look a bit like each parent, but are not identical to them.

Remember

Sexual reproduction can happen in plants as well as in animals.

Exam tip

Gametes have half the normal number of chromosomes. For example, human body cells have 46 chromosomes but human gametes have 23. Fertilisation produces a new cell with the normal number, in this case 46.

C Asexual reproduction

1 Asexual reproduction involves just one parent.

EY FACTS **2** There is *no fusion of gametes* in asexual reproduction. This means that there is *no mixing of genetic information* and the offspring are *identical* to the parent.

3 Genetically identical individuals are called clones. The parent and offspring are all clones.

PRACTICE QUESTIONS

1 Where are chromosomes found in the cell?
2 Explain why the offspring from sexual reproduction are not genetically identical to their parents.
3 Why does asexual reproduction produce clones?

THE BARE BONES

➤ Plants can be cloned quickly and cheaply by taking cuttings.
➤ There are several methods of modern cloning.
➤ Genetic engineering involves transferring genes from one organism to another.

A Cloning plants

KEY FACTS **1** Plants can be cloned by taking *cuttings*. New plants can be produced quickly and cheaply this way.

 A branch from the parent plant is cut off. Its lower leaves are removed and the stem is planted in damp compost.

 Plant hormones are used to encourage new roots to develop. The method is simple enough for most gardeners to do.

2 Plants can also be cloned by *tissue culture*.

3 Small groups of cells are taken from a part of the plant. They are added to *sterile agar jelly* containing nutrients and *plant hormones*. These encourage the cells to divide. Once the cells have grown into small masses of tissue, other hormones are added to stimulate the growth of roots and stems. The plantlets are then transferred into trays where they develop into plants.

KEY FACT **4** Tissue culture is more expensive and more difficult to do than taking cuttings.

B Cloning animals

KEY FACT **1** Animals can be cloned by *embryo transplants*, *fusion cell cloning* or by *adult cell cloning*.

KEY FACT

2 With embryo transplants, a *developing embryo* is removed from a pregnant animal. This is at an early stage before the cells have become specialised. The *cells are separated, grown in a laboratory* and then transplanted into *host mothers.*

embryo removed and split

placed in unfertilised eggs in separate cows

3 The offspring are identical to each other. They are genetically related to the original pregnant animal.
But they contain different genetic information from their host mothers.

4 Fusion cell cloning and adult cell cloning are similar to each other.
The main stages are:

- The nucleus of an unfertilised egg cell is removed.

- The nucleus from a different cell is injected into the egg cell.

- The egg cell is implanted into the womb of a host mother where it develops.

KEY FACT

5 In *fusion cell cloning* the donor nucleus comes from an *embryo.*
In *adult cell cloning* it comes from a *body cell* of an adult animal.

C Genetic engineering

1 Genetic engineering is also called genetic modification or GM.
Genetically modified organisms are called GMOs.

KEY FACT

2 Genes are 'cut out' of the chromosome of one cell using enzymes and transferred to another cell. This is usually from one species to another.
For example:

- bacteria have been produced that make human insulin

- crop plants have been developed that produce an insecticide.

PRACTICE QUESTIONS

1 Outline two ways in which plants can be cloned.

2 Explain why an animal produced by embryo transplant is not genetically identical to its host mother.

3 Geldings are male horses but they cannot reproduce. Describe how a valuable gelding racehorse could be cloned.

THE BARE BONES

➤ Fossils provide evidence that organisms have changed since life began on Earth.

➤ A species can become extinct for several reasons.

➤ The similarities and differences between species are analysed to learn about their evolutionary and ecological relationships.

A Fossils

1 A *fossil* is the *remains* of a *prehistoric animal or plant*, preserved in the Earth's crust. Usually, bones rather than soft parts are fossilised, but fossils can include footprints and other traces.

KEY FACT **2** Fossils give us evidence that living things have changed since life began on Earth. They may show that certain organisms have changed a lot, while others have changed very little.

3 Many fossil remains are of species that no longer exist. Such species have become *extinct*.

Remember

Fossil footprints may show whether an animal walked on two legs or four, and how fast it was walking.

B Extinction

1 The fossil record shows that many species have existed on Earth in the past but no longer exist. They have become **extinct**. *Extinction* happens when there are no living members of a certain species left.

KEY FACT **2** Extinction may be caused by factors such as:
- changes to the environment
- new competitors
- new diseases
- new predators.

Exam tip

Notice the use of the word 'new'. Remember that competitors, disease or predators are likely to be present all the time. It is the idea of a change that is important.

KEY FACT

1 The *theory of evolution* states that:
- simple life forms developed on Earth more than three billion years ago
- all species of living things have evolved from these life forms.

2 The *fossil record* provides evidence of evolution. But it has *gaps*. Not all organisms fossilise well. Many fossils will have been destroyed by natural movements of the Earth, or may not have been discovered yet.

3 There is a fairly complete evolutionary record of the *horse*. All the *main stages* of its evolution have been *preserved as fossils*. The horse evolved over 60 million years from a dog-sized creature that lived in rainforests into a tall animal adapted to living on the plains.

> **Exam tip**
>
> You may be given pictures or other information about fossils, and asked to explain how it relates to the theory of evolution.

PRACTICE QUESTIONS

1 What is a fossil?

2 A species of bird lives on an island. It nests on the ground. Explain why it might become extinct if rats escaped onto the island from a ship.

3 Outline the theory of evolution.

THE BARE BONES

➤ Darwin's theory of natural selection explained how evolution happens.
➤ There have been other theories of evolution.
➤ A species can change rapidly because of mutation.

A Natural selection

1 *Charles Darwin* was an English naturalist. He studied variation in plants and animals during a five-year voyage around the world in the 19th century. In 1859, Darwin published his ideas about evolution in a book called *On the Origin of Species*. He stated that evolution happens by natural selection.

KEY FACT

2 The main points about natural selection are:

• Individuals in a species show a wide range of variation (they are not all the same).

• This variation is caused by differences in their genes.

• Individuals with characteristics most suited to the environment are more likely to survive and reproduce.

• The genes that allow these individuals to be successful are passed to their offspring.

Remember

Scientists did not know about genes in Darwin's time. But they did know that offspring inherited their characteristics from their parents.

B Criticism of natural selection

KEY FACT

1 Darwin's theory of natural selection was only gradually accepted. There are many reasons for this.

2 We may never be certain about how life began on Earth. No-one was there to observe it or record observations.

3 Darwin's ideas caused a lot of controversy at the time, which still continues. His ideas can be seen as conflicting with *religious views* about the creation of the world and the living things in it.

4 Living things alive today are very *complex*. This is true even of microorganisms. Some people find it difficult to accept that this could have happened because of natural selection.

C Lamarck's theory of evolution

KEY FACT

1 There have been other theories of evolution.

2 Jean-Baptiste Lamarck was a French scientist who developed an alternative theory in the 19th century. It involved two ideas:

- A characteristic which is *used more* becomes *bigger and stronger.* One that is not used eventually disappears.

- Any feature that is *improved through use* is passed to the offspring.

Lamarck	Darwin
A giraffe stretches its neck to reach food high up	A giraffe with a longer neck can reach food high up
The giraffe's neck gets longer because it is used a lot	The giraffe is more likely to get enough food to survive to reproduce
The giraffe's offspring inherit its long neck	The giraffe's offspring inherit its long neck

Explaining the evolution of the giraffe's long neck using Lamarck's and Darwin's theories.

3 Lamarck's theory would predict that all species should become complex over time, and simple organisms would become extinct. Lamarck's theory cannot explain why simple organisms still exist today, but Darwin's theory can.

PRACTICE QUESTIONS

1 Outline the main points of natural selection.

2 Suggest a reason why Darwin's theory was accepted only gradually.

3 How can Darwin's theory of evolution explain why simple organisms such as bacteria exist, and have not all become extinct?

THE BARE BONES

➤ Human activities are using up raw materials and producing more waste.

➤ Waste can pollute the environment if it is not properly handled.

➤ Living organisms can be used as indicators of pollution.

A Impact of humans

KEY FACT **1** The *human population* is increasing rapidly and the *standard of living* for many people is improving. This *increase*s demands on the environment, including increases in:

- the use of non-renewable energy resources

- the use of raw materials, such as metal ores

- the amount of waste produced.

2 Humans are very successful competitors. We *compete* with other species for natural resources. *Farming*, *quarrying* and *building* reduce the amount of land available for plants and animals.

B Pollution

1 Human activities produce waste products, including solids, liquids and gases. These may be toxic and they may be difficult to dispose of. If waste is not handled properly it can cause pollution.

KEY FACTS **2** The air can be polluted with gases such as sulfur dioxide, and smoke. *Sulfur dioxide* contributes to *acid rain*. This damages buildings, living things in rivers and lakes, and trees. Smoke blackens buildings and can make it difficult for us to breathe.

3 The land can be polluted with *toxic chemicals*. These include *herbicides* (weedkillers) and *pesticides* used by farmers to improve their crop yields. The rain can wash these chemicals into rivers, lakes and seas.

EY FACT **4** Rivers, lakes and seas can be polluted with toxic chemicals from factories, fertilisers and pesticides from fields, and *sewage*.

Remember

Sewage may contain harmful microorganisms that can cause disease.

> **Exam tip**
>
> Look out for questions that might involve knowledge and understanding from another area of science. For example, most plastics are not biodegradable. They are often dumped in landfill sites.

C Indicators of pollution

1 Living things are often very sensitive to pollution in their environment. It may be difficult for them to survive if certain polluting chemicals are there. Scientists can find out how polluted the environment is by analysing the species present.

EY FACTS **2** *Invertebrate animals* such as insect larvae can be used to *indicate pollution in water*. Clean rivers and lakes contain more species, and bigger populations, of invertebrates than polluted rivers and lakes.

3 *Lichens* are a type of plant that grows on walls and trees. They absorb water and minerals over their entire surface area from the rain and the air. This makes them *sensitive to air pollution*. Lichens grow well in unpolluted air, but there may be very few growing in towns.

Remember

Sustainable development involves meeting our needs without damaging the ability of future generations to meet their own needs. We need to manage our use of resources at local, regional and worldwide levels.

PRACTICE QUESTIONS

1 Explain why the use of non-renewable energy resources is increasing.

2 Outline one way in which farming can pollute the environment.

3 Explain why walls in towns may have few lichens growing on them, but walls in the countryside may have many lichens.

4 Suggest why it is important for future generations that we recycle metals.

THE BARE BONES

➤ Greenhouse gases such as carbon dioxide and methane absorb heat energy in the atmosphere.

➤ Human activities are increasing the amounts of greenhouse gases in the atmosphere.

➤ Increasing amounts of greenhouse gases may be causing global warming.

➤ Global warming may cause climate change and a rise in sea level.

A Greenhouse effect

1 The Earth's surface radiates *thermal energy*. Without an atmosphere this thermal energy would escape into space and the planet would be much colder than it is.

KEY FACTS **2** Carbon dioxide and methane are greenhouse gases.
They *absorb* most of the *thermal energy* radiated by the Earth.

3 Some of this energy is radiated *back to the Earth*. It keeps the planet *warmer* than it would be without the greenhouse gases. This is called the greenhouse effect.

B Global warming

1 Human activities are releasing large, extra amounts of greenhouse gases into the atmosphere.

KEY FACTS **2** Increasing levels of greenhouse gases increase the greenhouse effect.
This in turn increases the average temperature of the planet.
This is called global warming.

3 Global warming by only a few degrees Celsius may cause:

• a rise in sea levels

• large-scale changes to the weather, called climate change.

C Methane

1 *Methane* is released into the atmosphere because of *farming*. It is produced by *rice paddy fields* and by *cattle*.

2 The world's population is increasing. This means that there are increasing numbers of cattle and rice paddy fields. In turn, this means that increasing amounts of methane are released into the atmosphere.

D Carbon dioxide

1 *Trees* are being *cut down* in tropical areas of the world. This *deforestation* provides *timber* for building, and *land* for farming.

2 Deforestation leads to a loss of *biodiversity*. Some of the species that become extinct might have been useful to us in the future. For example, they might have been a source of new medicines.

3 Deforestation also adds to the amount of carbon dioxide in the atmosphere, leading to global warming:

- there are fewer trees left to absorb carbon dioxide from the atmosphere

- fallen trees may be burnt, and this releases carbon dioxide

- decay microorganisms release carbon dioxide.

PRACTICE QUESTIONS

1 What is a greenhouse gas?

2 Describe one problem that could be caused by global warming.

3 Explain how farming can increase the amount of methane and carbon dioxide released into the atmosphere.

THE BARE BONES

➤ All substances are made from tiny particles called atoms.
➤ An element is a substance made from just one sort of atom.
➤ The elements are shown in the periodic table.
➤ Groups in the periodic table contain elements with similar properties.

A Atoms

1 All substances are made of atoms.

KEY FACT **2** There is a small nucleus at the centre of each atom, with even smaller particles called electrons arranged around it.

B Elements

KEY FACT **1** There are about 100 different elements. Each element is made of just one sort of atom. Different elements are made from different sorts of atom.

2 Each element is given a chemical symbol. For example, the symbol for magnesium is Mg and the symbol for oxygen is O.

Chemical symbols for the elements are made from one, two or three letters. The first letter is always a capital letter, and the next one or two are lower case.

Exam tip

1 The periodic table is a chart showing information about the elements.

2 The vertical columns in the periodic table are called groups. The elements in a group have similar properties to each other.

Remember

You won't find substances like water and carbon dioxide in the periodic table because they are *compounds*, not elements.

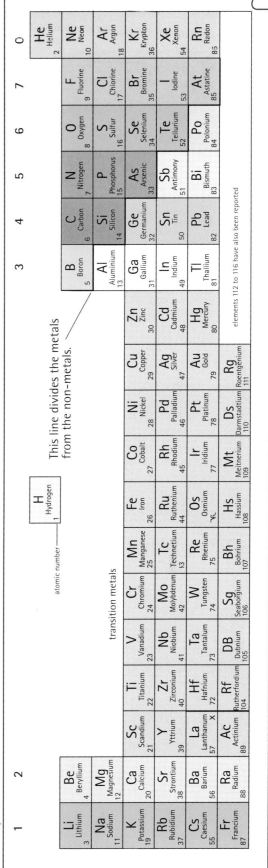

Group 1 is called the alkali metals, group 2 is called the alkaline earth metals, group 7 is called the halogens, and group 0 is called the noble gases.

This line divides the metals from the non-metals.

transition metals

atomic number ——— H Hydrogen 1

PRACTICE QUESTIONS

1 Describe the structure of the atom.

2 What is an element?

3 Explain what a group is in the periodic table.

THE BARE BONES

> ➤ Atoms join together to form compounds in chemical reactions.
> ➤ Chemical bonds join atoms together.
> ➤ A chemical formula shows the number of atoms of each element in a compound.
> ➤ A balanced chemical equation shows what happens to each substance in a chemical reaction.

A Chemical reactions

1 In a chemical reaction, the substances that react together are called reactants and the substances that are produced are called products.

KEY FACT **2** In a chemical reaction, the atoms in the reactants join together in a different way than before to make the products.

3 The joins between atoms are called chemical bonds. They form when electrons move from one atom to another, or are shared between two atoms.

You don't need to know any more than this about chemical bonds for GCSE Science. You will find out more about them if you study GCSE Additional Science.

Exam tip

B Chemical formulae

KEY FACT **1** A chemical formula shows the number of each type of atom in a compound.

For example:

• H_2O is the formula for water. It shows that a molecule of water contains two hydrogen atoms and one oxygen atom.

• CO_2 is the formula for carbon dioxide. It shows that a molecule of carbon dioxide contains one carbon atom and two oxygen atoms.

Remember

The numbers in chemical formulae are subscripts. So CO_2 is correct but CO^2 is not.

C Conservation of mass

Limestone

THE BARE BONES

➤ Limestone contains calcium carbonate. It is used as a building material and as a raw material for making other substances.

➤ Calcium carbonate decomposes when heated, forming calcium oxide and carbon dioxide.

➤ Calcium oxide reacts with water to form calcium hydroxide.

A Limestone

KEY FACT

1 Limestone is a common rock found in many parts of the UK.
It is mostly calcium carbonate, $CaCO_3$.

2 Limestone is removed from the ground in quarries.

3 Blocks of limestone are used as a building material.
Crushed limestone chippings are used for road building.

B Thermal decomposition

KEY FACT

1 Calcium carbonate breaks down to form calcium oxide and carbon dioxide when it is heated strongly:

calcium carbonate → calcium oxide + carbon dioxide

$CaCO_3 \rightarrow CaO + CO_2$

This reaction is called thermal decomposition.

2 Other metal carbonates react in a similar way. For example, green copper carbonate decomposes when heated to form black copper oxide:

copper carbonate → copper oxide + carbon dioxide

$CuCO_3 \rightarrow CuO + CO_2$

C Quicklime and slaked lime

1 Calcium oxide is also called quicklime. Its chemical formula is CaO.

2 Calcium oxide reacts with water to produce calcium hydroxide, also called slaked lime. The formula of calcium hydroxide is $Ca(OH)_2$.

KEY FACT 3 Using common names instead of chemical names, this is how limestone is changed by chemical reactions:

- limestone $\xrightarrow{\text{heat}}$ quicklime + carbon dioxide
- quicklime + water → slaked lime.

D Uses of limestone and its products

1 Limestone is:

- used to remove impurities when iron is extracted from iron ore
- heated with sand and sodium carbonate to make glass
- heated with clay to make cement.

2 Cement is:

- mixed with sand and water to make mortar
- mixed with sand, water and crushed rock to make concrete.

3 Limestone, quicklime and slaked lime are used to reduce the acidity of fields and lakes affected by acid rain.

PRACTICE QUESTIONS

1 Limestone quarries are often located in countryside areas, which may also be tourist areas. Outline some of the advantages and disadvantages of quarrying limestone.

2 Suggest why the demand for limestone increases when a large building project starts, such as the 2012 London Olympic Games.

THE BARE BONES

➤ Ores are rocks that contain useful amounts of metal.

➤ Chemical reactions are needed to extract most metals from their ores.

➤ Metals that are less reactive than carbon, such as iron, are extracted from their ores by reduction with carbon.

A Ores

KEY FACT **1** Ores are naturally occurring rocks that contain enough metal to make it economical to extract the metal.

2 Common ores include haematite (iron ore) and bauxite (aluminium ore).

3 High-grade ores contain a lot of the desired metal, and low-grade ores contain very little of it. Many of the world's high-grade ores have already been mined.

4 There is a limited supply of ores. Recycling metals after use reduces the need to mine ores and it saves energy.

B Methods of extraction

KEY FACT **1** Unreactive metals are found in the Earth's crust as the metal itself. Gold is like this. But most metals need chemical reactions to extract them from their ores.

2 Many metals are found in their ores as oxides. The metals are extracted by removing the oxygen. This is called reduction.

3 The method of chemical extraction depends on how reactive the metal is:

• Metals that are less reactive than carbon can be extracted from their oxides by reduction with carbon or carbon monoxide.

• Metals that are more reactive than carbon are extracted using electricity.

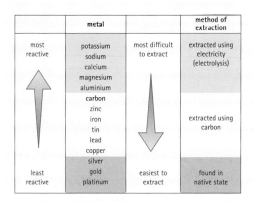

Part of the reactivity series of metals
and the method of extraction.

	metal		method of extraction
most reactive	potassium sodium calcium magnesium aluminium	most difficult to extract	extracted using electricity (electrolysis)
	carbon		
	zinc iron tin lead copper		extracted using carbon
	silver		
least reactive	gold platinum	easiest to extract	found in native state

Exam tip

You will be given a copy of the reactivity series on a **Data Sheet** in written exams. You will be given enough information to help you answer multiple-choice questions.

C Iron

KEY FACT **1** Iron is less reactive than carbon, so it can be extracted from iron oxide by reduction using carbon.

2 Iron is extracted from iron oxide in a large container called a blast furnace. These are the equations for one of the reactions that take place there:

iron oxide + carbon → iron + carbon dioxide

$$2Fe_2O_3 + 3C \rightarrow 4Fe + 3CO_2$$

KEY FACT **3** Iron straight from the blast furnace contains about 96% iron. The remaining 4% is impurities such as carbon. These make the iron hard but brittle. This means it breaks easily when stretched or bent, so it has few uses. It may be used for some cooking stoves.

Exam tip

You don't need to know any details of the blast furnace for your exams.

PRACTICE QUESTIONS

1 What is an ore?

2 Explain why you could extract lead from lead oxide by reduction with carbon, but you could not extract aluminium from aluminium oxide this way.

3 Why does iron straight from the blast furnace have few uses?

THE BARE BONES

➤ Alloys are mixtures of a metal with non-metals or other metals.

➤ Alloys can be designed to have properties that make them suited for certain uses.

➤ Smart alloys go back to their original shape after being bent.

A Pure metals

KEY FACTS

1 The atoms in *pure metals* are *regularly arranged*. Layers of atoms can slide over each other.

2 Iron straight from the blast furnace is brittle because of its impurities. If all the impurities were removed, the pure iron would be soft and easily shaped. This is because layers of iron atoms could slide over each other.

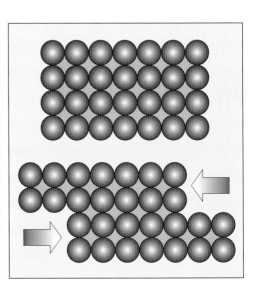

Pure iron is soft because layers of atoms slide over each other easily.

B Steel

KEY FACT

1 Pure iron would be too soft for many uses, so most iron is converted into steel.

2 Steel is made by removing most of the carbon from iron from the blast furnace, then adding other metals to make alloys.
There are different types of steel, including:

• low carbon steel that is easily shaped – useful for making car body panels

• high carbon steel that is hard – useful for making tools

• stainless steel that is resistant to corrosion – useful for sinks and cutlery.

1 Alloys contain different-sized atoms. These alter the regular arrangement of atoms so that the layers cannot slide over each other easily. This means that alloys are harder than the pure metal.

2 Different alloys can be designed with different properties. This makes them useful for particular purposes, and many everyday metals are alloys. For example:

- Copper is alloyed with zinc to make brass, which is used in electrical fittings.

- Gold is alloyed with copper for use in jewellery.

- Aluminium is alloyed with copper and other metals to make duralumin, which is used in aircraft parts.

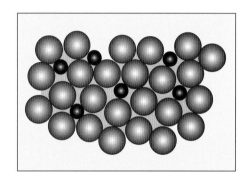

It is more difficult for layers of atoms to slide over each other easily in alloys.

D Smart alloys

1 **Smart alloys** are mixtures of metals such as nickel and titanium that have unusual properties. For example, they spring back into shape after being bent.

2 *Shape memory alloys* are smart alloys which can be twisted and bent, but snap back into shape when they are warmed up.

PRACTICE QUESTIONS

1 What is an alloy?

2 Explain why alloys are harder than the pure metals they contain.

3 Suggest why high carbon steel would not be suitable for making car body panels.

THE BARE BONES

➤ The elements in the middle block of the periodic table are called the transition metals.

➤ Many of the transition metals are useful as construction metals.

➤ Supplies of copper ore are limited.

➤ It is expensive to extract titanium and aluminium.

A The transition metals

KEY FACT **1** The transition metals are the elements in the central block of the periodic table, between group 2 and group 3. They include metals such as iron, copper and titanium.

2 The transition metals have the typical properties of metals. They:

- are good conductors of heat

- are good conductors of electricity

- can be hammered or bent into shape.

transition metals

3 Many transition metals are strong and tough. They are useful as *structural materials*, for example for making office blocks, bridges, vehicles and ships.

B Copper

KEY FACT **1** Most of the high-grade copper ores have already been mined, so they are in limited supply. Most copper is now extracted from low-grade ores. These contain relatively little copper. This means that a lot of waste is produced when they are mined and the copper is extracted.

2 Copper can be extracted by passing electricity through dilute solutions of copper compounds, such as copper sulfate. This is called electrolysis.

3 Electrolysis is expensive because large amounts of electricity are needed. But other metals are recovered in the waste sludge, such as silver. This helps to offset the cost, but not the environmental impact.

4 New ways to extract copper are being researched, including using bacteria.

use of copper	reasons for using copper
plumbing (water pipes and fittings)	does not react with water easily bent into shape without breaking
electrical cables	easily made into wires a good conductor of electricity

Some uses of copper and reasons for using it.

C Titanium

1 Titanium is a transition metal. Its surface is protected from corrosion by a layer of titanium oxide. It is strong and has a low density, so objects made from titanium are lightweight for their size. Titanium is used for aircraft parts and artificial hip joints.

EY FACT **2** Titanium cannot be extracted by reducing titanium oxide using carbon. It is expensive to extract titanium because several steps are needed, and each needs a lot of energy.

D Aluminium

1 Aluminium is not a transition metal. It is found in group 3. But, like titanium, its surface is protected from corrosion by a layer of its oxide, and it has a low density.

EY FACT **2** Aluminium is more reactive than carbon, so it cannot be extracted by reducing aluminium oxide using carbon. It is expensive to extract aluminium because it is extracted by electrolysis, which needs a lot of energy.

Remember

It is better to recycle metals than to extract them from their ores. It saves energy, preserves the limited supplies of ores, and has less impact on the environment.

PRACTICE QUESTIONS

1 What makes copper useful for plumbing?
2 Explain why it is expensive to extract titanium and aluminium from their ores.
3 Scientists have discovered a new way to extract titanium in one step.
Suggest why this should make titanium more widely available in the future.

Hydrocarbons

THE BARE BONES

➤ Crude oil is a mixture of hydrocarbons.

➤ Hydrocarbons are compounds of hydrogen and carbon.

➤ Alkanes are hydrocarbons with the general formula C_nH_{2n+2}.

➤ The different hydrocarbons in crude oil can be separated by fractional distillation.

A Crude oil

1 Crude oil is a fossil fuel.

KEY FACT **2** Crude oil contains a large number of hydrocarbons.
These are compounds containing hydrogen and carbon only.

B Alkanes

KEY FACT **1** Alkanes are the simplest hydrocarbons. The general formula of alkanes is C_nH_{2n+2}. This means that, for example, the molecular formula for ethane is C_2H_6.

2 Alkanes are saturated compounds. This means that all the bonds in alkanes are *single bonds*. The atoms in an alkane and how they are joined together can be shown by a structural formula.

name	molecular formula	structural formula
methane	CH_4	H—C—H with H above and H below
ethane	C_2H_6	H—C—C—H with H's above and below
propane	C_3H_8	H—C—C—C—H with H's above and below
butane	C_4H_{10}	H—C—C—C—C—H with H's above and below

The molecular formulae and structural formulae of the first four alkanes.

C Fractional distillation

1 The longer the alkane, the higher its boiling point. The different boiling points of alkanes allow crude oil to be separated into fractions by fractional distillation. They are called *fractions* because they are only a *part* of the original crude oil.

EY FACT 2 Fractional distillation works by heating the crude oil to evaporate it, then letting it condense at several different temperatures:

- gases leave the top of the fractionating column

- liquids leave at various levels in the middle

- solids stay at the bottom.

D Different fractions

EY FACT 1 Shorter alkanes make better fuels than longer alkanes. This is because the shorter the hydrocarbon molecule:

- the lower its boiling point (the more volatile it is)

- the runnier it is (its viscosity is lower)

- the easier it is to ignite.

PRACTICE QUESTIONS

1 What is a hydrocarbon?

2 Write the molecular formula of hexane, which contains six carbon atoms.

3 Explain how crude oil can be separated into fractions.

4 Explain why fractions from the top half of the fractionating column are more useful as fuels than those from the bottom half.

Burning fuels

THE BARE BONES

> ➤ Hydrocarbons burn in air to produce water vapour and carbon dioxide.
> ➤ Many fuels contain some sulfur, which produces sulfur dioxide when the fuel is burned.
> ➤ The products from burning fuels damage the environment.
> ➤ Sulfur can be removed from fuels before their use, and sulfur dioxide can be removed from waste gases.

A Complete combustion

1 Fuels react with oxygen in the air when they burn. The reaction is called combustion. When there is plenty of air, burning is called *complete* combustion.

KEY FACT **2** The hydrogen in hydrocarbons forms water vapour when the fuel burns. The carbon in coal and hydrocarbons forms carbon dioxide when the fuel burns in plenty of air.

3 The general word equations for complete combustion are:

- carbon + oxygen → carbon dioxide   (for coal)
- hydrocarbon + oxygen → water vapour + carbon dioxide.

4 The balanced symbol equations for some hydrocarbons burning are:

- $CH_4 + 2O_2 \rightarrow CO_2 + 2H_2O$ (for natural gas)
- $C_4H_{10} + 6\frac{1}{2}O_2 \rightarrow 4CO_2 + 5H_2O$ (for butane).

B Incomplete combustion

KEY FACT **1** *Incomplete* combustion happens when there is a poor supply of air. Poisonous *carbon monoxide* gas is produced instead of carbon dioxide. *Particles* of carbon (smoke and soot) may also be produced.

C Pollution from burning fuels

KEY FACTS

1 Carbon dioxide is a *greenhouse gas*. It prevents heat energy escaping from the atmosphere and contributes to *global warming*. If there is less demand for fossil fuels, the amount of carbon dioxide released will go down. This will reduce global warming.

2 Particles cause global dimming. They increase the cloud cover, which reduces the amount of sunlight reaching the ground. Laws requiring smokeless fuels help to reduce the amount of particles released.

3 *Alternative fuels* such as ethanol and hydrogen may reduce these pollutants. Ethanol produced by fermentation of sugars can be a *carbon neutral fuel*. Water vapour is the only product formed when hydrogen burns.

Remember
Ethanol will not be a carbon neutral fuel if some of the energy needed to produce it comes from fossil fuels.

> Don't confuse greenhouse gases and global warming with damage to the ozone layer.
>
> **Exam tip**

D Acid rain

KEY FACTS

1 Sulfur dioxide from burning fuels contributes to *acid rain*.
Fuels can be processed to remove the sulfur before they are used.

2 Sulfur dioxide can be removed from waste gases, for example at power stations. One way to do this involves spraying powdered limestone into the waste gases. A reaction happens that produces gypsum, which is used to make plasterboard.

PRACTICE QUESTIONS

1 Name five products of combustion.

2 What is the difference between complete combustion and incomplete combustion?

3 Some scientists believe that global dimming has helped to reduce global warming over the last few decades. Suggest what could happen as technology improves and fewer particles are emitted when fuels are used.

Alkenes

THE BARE BONES

➤ Alkenes are hydrocarbons that contain a carbon–carbon double bond.

➤ Alkenes have the general formula C_nH_{2n}.

➤ Alkenes can be produced by cracking crude oil fractions.

➤ Ethanol can be produced by reacting ethene with steam.

A Alkenes

KEY FACTS

1 Alkenes are hydrocarbons with the general formula C_nH_{2n}.
This means that, for example, the *molecular formula* for ethene is C_2H_4.

2 Alkenes are unsaturated compounds.
This means that they contain a double bond.

3 Alkenes decolourise brown bromine water, but alkanes do not.

ethene C_2H_4 propene C_3H_6 butene C_4H_8

$$\begin{array}{ccc} H & H \\ | & | \\ C & = & C \\ | & | \\ H & H \end{array}$$

The molecular formulae and structural formulae of the first three alkenes.

Exam tip

Take care that your letter e does not look a letter a, otherwise the word alkene will look like alkane when you write it.

B Cracking

KEY FACT

1 The *demand* for shorter alkanes is greater than can be supplied by fractional distillation alone. Cracking is a process in which long alkanes are broken down into shorter alkanes and alkenes. The shorter alkanes are useful as fuels.

KEY FACT **2** Cracking is an example of a *thermal decomposition* reaction. Alkanes are heated so that they vaporise, which is then passed over a hot **catalyst**, such as aluminium oxide.

3 Here is an example of the equations for a cracking reaction:

decane → octane + ethene

$$C_{10}H_{22} \rightarrow C_8H_{18} + C_2H_4$$

Remember
Another thermal decomposition reaction is the breakdown of metal carbonates to metal oxides and carbon dioxide.

C Ethanol

KEY FACT **1** Ethene reacts with steam at high temperatures and pressures to form ethanol, C_2H_5OH. A catalyst of phosphoric acid is needed, too.

2 Ethanol is the only product in the reaction:

ethene + steam → ethanol

$$C_2H_4 + H_2O \rightarrow C_2H_5OH$$

$$\underset{\substack{| \;\; | \\ H \;\; H}}{\overset{\substack{H \;\; H \\ | \;\; |}}{C=C}} + \underset{H \quad H}{\overset{O}{\wedge}} \rightarrow H-\underset{\substack{| \;\; | \\ H \;\; H}}{\overset{\substack{H \;\; H \\ | \;\; |}}{C-C}}-OH$$

Diagram to illustrate how ethanol is produced by reacting ethene with steam.

3 Ethanol can be produced from **renewable resources** by fermentation of sugars from plant materials. It is often called *bioethanol*.

KEY FACT **4** The use of bioethanol as a fuel reduces the demand for fossil fuels. But it uses farm land that could have been used to grow crops to feed people.

PRACTICE QUESTIONS

1 What is cracking and why is it carried out?

2 Write the molecular formula for hexene, an alkene with six carbon atoms.

3 Suggest why the alcohol for beer and wine is ethanol from fermentation, rather than ethanol from the reaction between ethene and steam.

THE BARE BONES

➤ Alkenes can join together to make very long molecules called polymers.

➤ The properties of polymers depend on what they were made from and the conditions used.

➤ Polymers have very many uses but can be difficult to dispose of once they have been used.

A Monomers and polymers

1 Alkenes can join together because they contain a carbon–carbon double bond.

KEY FACT **2** When alkenes join together to make polymers, they are called monomers. Different monomers make different polymers. For example, ethene makes poly(ethene) and propene makes poly(propene).

3 Polymers have many uses, including:

- plastic bags

- dental fillings

- *shape memory polymers* for shrink-wrap packaging

- *hydrogels* for making soft disposable nappies and contact lenses.

$$\underset{\underset{H}{\overset{CH_3}{|}}}{C} = \underset{\underset{H}{|}}{C} + \underset{\underset{H}{\overset{CH_3}{|}}}{C} = \underset{\underset{H}{|}}{C} + \underset{\underset{H}{\overset{CH_3}{|}}}{C} = \underset{\underset{H}{|}}{C}$$

$$\downarrow$$

$$-\underset{\underset{H}{\overset{CH_3}{|}}}{C} - \underset{\underset{H}{|}}{C} - \underset{\underset{H}{\overset{CH_3}{|}}}{C} - \underset{\underset{H}{|}}{C} - \underset{\underset{H}{\overset{CH_3}{|}}}{C} - \underset{\underset{H}{|}}{C} -$$

Propene monomers *polymerise* to make poly(propene).

B Properties of polymers

KEY FACT **1** The properties of polymers depend on what they were made from and the conditions used.

2 Polymer molecules can have more or fewer branches, depending on the conditions used to make them.

polymer	branches	relative strength	maximum useable temperature /°C
LDPE low-density poly(ethene)	many	weak	85
HDPE high-density poly(ethene)	few	strong	120

The properties of poly(ethene) depend upon the amount of branching.

3 Substances called *plasticisers* allow polymer molecules to slide over each other more easily. PVC with plasticisers is soft and flexible. It is used for floor coverings and raincoats. But unplasticised PVC or uPVC is hard. It is used to make pipes and window frames.

4 Poly(ethenol) is a polymer that dissolves in water to make slime. Its viscosity depends on the proportions of the ingredients used to make it.

> **Exam tip**
>
> You may be given information in the exam about the properties of some polymers. Use this with your knowledge and understanding of science to answer the question.

D Disposing of polymers

EY FACTS **1** Biodegradable polymers can be broken down by microorganisms.

2 Many polymers are *not biodegradable*. They take a very long time to break down. This makes them difficult to dispose of once they have been used.

PRACTICE QUESTIONS

1 Name the polymer formed from chloroethene monomers.

2 Use information from the table to explain which polymer, LDPE or HDPE, would be best for making disposable hot drinks cups.

3 Suggest why the cost of polymers often depends on the cost of crude oil.

Plant oils

THE BARE BONES

➤ Some fruit, seeds and nuts contain vegetable oils that can be extracted.
➤ Vegetable oils are an important part of our diet, and can be used as fuels.
➤ Emulsions are mixtures of oils and water, as used in salad dressings.
➤ Unsaturated vegetable oils can be hardened by reacting them with hydrogen.

A Extracting vegetable oils

KEY FACTS

1 Vegetable oils are natural oils found in some fruit, seeds and nuts.

2 Oils can be extracted by:
- crushing the plant material
- pressing the crushed material to squeeze out the oil
- removing impurities such as water.

3 Oils can also be extracted by:
- dissolving the oil in a solvent
- distilling to remove the solvent.

B Uses of vegetable oils

KEY FACTS

1 Vegetable oils are an important part of a *balanced diet*. They are a source of *energy*. They also contain vitamins and other nutrients.

2 Vegetable oils are also used as *fuels for vehicles*. For example, *biodiesel* is extracted from oilseed rape plants or from used cooking oil.

advantages	disadvantages
reduces the use of fossil fuels	reduces the amount of land available for growing food crops
can be a carbon-neutral fuel	energy from fossil fuels may be needed to produce and transport it

Some advantages and disadvantages of using vegetable oils as fuels.

Remember
A carbon-neutral fuel does not add extra carbon dioxide to the atmosphere when it is used.

C Vegetable oils in food

KEY FACT **1** Vegetable oils do not dissolve in water, but they can form mixtures called *emulsions*. These are *more viscous* (thicker and less runny) than oil or water.

2 *Emulsifiers* are substances that prevent the oil and water in an emulsion from separating again.

KEY FACT **3** Emulsions improve the *appearance* and *texture* of food. They are used in foods such as ice cream and salad dressings.

D Hardening vegetable oils

KEY FACTS **1** Unsaturated vegetable oils contain carbon–carbon double bonds. These can be detected using bromine or iodine. The more double bonds, the more bromine or iodine reacts.

2 Unsaturated vegetable oils are usually liquids at room temperature. They can be **hardened** by reacting them with *hydrogen* at about 60 °C. A nickel catalyst is needed too.

Hydrogen adds across a carbon–carbon double bond, forming a carbon–carbon single bond.

3 Hardened oils are more saturated. They are called **hydrogenated vegetable oils**. They have higher melting points than unsaturated vegetable oils. This means that they:

- are solid at room temperature
- are useful in margarine
- can be used to make pastries and cakes.

PRACTICE QUESTIONS

1 Outline the steps to extract a vegetable oil.

2 Why do we need vegetable oils in our diet?

3 What is an emulsion, and where might you find one in food?

4 Describe how vegetable oils are hardened, and explain why this is done.

Food additives

THE BARE BONES

➤ Additives are put into food to improve its taste, appearance and shelf-life.

➤ Permitted additives are given E numbers.

➤ Additives can be identified by chemical analysis.

➤ Chromatography can be used to detect and identify artificial colours.

A Food additives

KEY FACTS

1 Food additives are included in processed foods to improve:

- taste

- appearance

- shelf-life (how long the food lasts when stored).

2 Food additives must be identified in the *list of ingredients* on the packet. Some are *natural* and some are *artificial*.

3 Some additives have an E number. This means that they have been *tested for safety*, passed for use in food and licensed by the European Union.

type of additive	example	typical use
colouring	E102 (tartrazine)	orange colouring for soft drinks and sweets
preservative	E210 (benzoic acid)	stops harmful microorganisms growing
emulsifier	E322 (lecithin)	allows oil and water to form emulsions for ice cream and salad dressings
sweetener	E951 (aspartame)	low-calorie food and drink sweetening

Some food additives and why they are used in food.

B Risks of food additives

1 Some additives can cause allergic reactions in some people. For example, the UK *Food Standards Agency* has strict limits on the amount of colourings allowed in food. They are banned from baby foods.

2 Banned substances have been added to food by mistake. For example, a red dye called *Sudan I* caused a food scare in 2005. It was used in chilli powder before it was banned. Some of this chilli powder was later used in food by mistake, and hundreds of food items had to be removed and destroyed.

> **Exam tip**
>
> You may be asked to evaluate the benefits and drawbacks of food additives using information about them.

C Analysing food

EY FACTS **1** Additives in food can be identified by chemical analysis.

2 **Chromatography** is used to detect and identify artificial food colourings.

Remember
Modern chromatography in analytical laboratories is automated to get fast, accurate results from tiny samples.

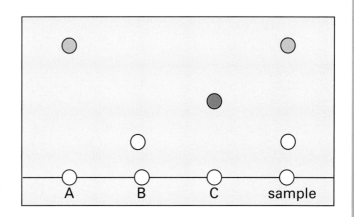

The sample in this chromatogram contains food colourings A and B, but not C.

PRACTICE QUESTIONS

1 Give two reasons why processed food may contain additives.
2 How do you know if food contains additives?
3 Describe a risk of artificial food additives.

THE BARE BONES

➤ The Earth consists of a core, mantle and crust.
➤ The crust and upper part of the mantle are broken into tectonic plates.
➤ Tectonic plates move very slowly.
➤ Earthquakes and volcanoes happen where plates meet.

A Structure of the Earth

KEY FACT **1** The Earth consists of several layers, the core, mantle and crust.

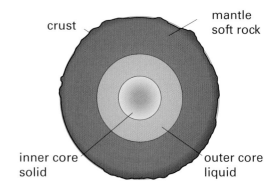

crust
mantle soft rock
inner core solid
outer core liquid

2 The core consists of iron and nickel. The *outer core* is liquid but the *inner core* is solid.

3 The mantle is made from rock, but this can *flow* very slowly.

4 The crust is made from solid rock. It is the *thinnest layer*, about 50 km deep.

B Plate tectonics

KEY FACTS **1** The Earth's crust and the *upper part of the mantle* are broken into huge pieces called tectonic plates.

2 *Convection currents* in the mantle are driven by heat produced from *radioactive processes* deep inside the Earth. These currents cause the plates to move at a few centimetres per year.

3 Where tectonic plates meet, the Earth's crust becomes unstable. The plates push against each other, or move over and under each other. Earthquakes and volcanic eruptions happen at the boundaries between plates.

4 Although areas of plate boundaries are known for earthquakes and volcanoes, it is difficult to predict exactly when these might happen and how bad they will be.

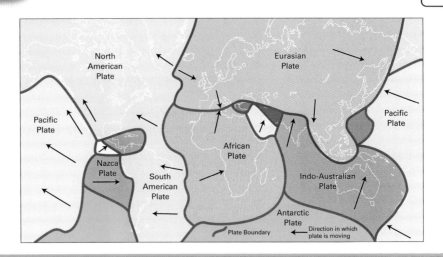

C Evidence for plate tectonics

KEY FACT **1** At one time scientists thought that mountains and other features on the Earth's surface happened because the crust shrank as the Earth cooled.

2 One problem with this theory is it does not explain why mountains only occur in certain places, and not all over the Earth's surface.

3 Alfred Wegener in the early part of the last century proposed the theory of continental drift involving tectonic plates. His evidence included:

• The east coast of South America and the west coast of Africa fit together like jigsaw pieces.

• Similar rocks and fossils are found on both continents.

This suggested that the two continents were once part of a single land mass which had moved apart.

KEY FACT **4** Wegener's theory explained why mountains occur in certain places, at plate boundaries. But he could not explain how tectonic plates could move. His theory was not generally accepted by scientists for many years, until sufficient evidence was collected.

PRACTICE QUESTIONS

1 Describe the structure of the Earth.

2 State one problem with the idea that shrinkage of the crust caused mountains.

3 Outline two pieces of evidence for plate tectonics.

4 Where do earthquakes and volcanoes happen?

THE BARE BONES

➤ The Earth's atmosphere is about 80% nitrogen and 20% oxygen, with small proportions of other gases such as water vapour, carbon dioxide and noble gases.

➤ The early atmosphere was mostly carbon dioxide.

➤ Plants produced the oxygen that is in the atmosphere.

A The modern atmosphere

KEY FACT **1** The Earth's atmosphere has stayed roughly the same for the last 200 million years:

- 78% nitrogen
- 21% oxygen
- 0.9% argon (a noble gas)
- 0.1% of other gases, such as carbon dioxide and water vapour.

> You may be asked to complete a pie chart to show the proportions of the main gases. Notice that nitrogen is about 80% and oxygen about 20%.

Exam tip

B The early atmosphere

1 The atmospheres of Mars and Venus today are mostly carbon dioxide with little or no oxygen. Theories about the history of the Earth suggest that the Earth's atmosphere was like this to begin with.

KEY FACT **2** During the first billion years after the Earth formed, intense volcanic activity released gases. These became the early atmosphere. This was mostly carbon dioxide with some water vapour, methane and ammonia.

3 As the Earth cooled, water vapour from the early atmosphere condensed to form the oceans.

Remember

Theories about the evolution of the atmosphere must be able to explain why carbon dioxide decreased, and oxygen and nitrogen increased.

C Evolution of the atmosphere

KEY FACTS **1** Plants evolved. *Photosynthesis* by plants produced the oxygen in the atmosphere and continues to do so today.

2 Carbon dioxide decreased because it:
- *dissolved* in the oceans
- was taken in by plants and eventually became *fossil fuels*
- formed *carbonates* in *sedimentary rocks* such as limestone (calcium carbonate).

3 Methane and ammonia decreased because they reacted with oxygen. Nitrogen increased because of the reaction of ammonia with oxygen, and the action of certain bacteria.

D Carbon dioxide

KEY FACT **1** The level of carbon dioxide in the atmosphere is increasing.
The burning of fossil fuels is adding carbon dioxide to the atmosphere faster than it can be removed.

PRACTICE QUESTIONS

1 What was the main gas in the early atmosphere?
2 What is the main gas in the modern atmosphere?
3 Outline the reasons why carbon dioxide in the atmosphere decreased and oxygen increased.
4 Suggest why these ideas about the evolution of the atmosphere are described as theories, rather than facts.

Noble gases

THE BARE BONES

➤ The noble gases are found in group 0 of the periodic table.

➤ They are all chemically unreactive.

➤ The noble gases are used in light bulbs and advertising signs.

➤ Helium is less dense than air, so it is used as a lifting gas in balloons.

A The noble gases

KEY FACT **1** The noble gases are the elements in group 0 of the periodic table.

2 Group 0 is found on the far right hand side of the periodic table. It includes:

- helium
- neon
- argon
- krypton
- xenon
- radon.

The noble gases are placed in the far right hand column of the periodic table.

B Properties of the noble gases

KEY FACT **1** The noble gases are all:

- non-metals
- gases at room temperature
- chemically unreactive.

Exam tip

If an element's name ends in 'um' it is a metal. There is one exception: helium is a non-metal.

C Uses of the noble gases

EY FACT **1** Argon is used in *filament lamps* (ordinary light bulbs).

2 There is a very thin metal wire inside filament lamps which gets hot and glows. When unreactive argon replaces air in the lamp, it stops the wire burning away.

EY FACT **3** The noble gases *glow* when high voltage electricity is passed through them. They are used in *electric discharge tubes*, used for 'neon' advertising signs.

D Helium as a lifting gas

Y FACT **1** Helium is *much less dense* than air, so it can be used as a *lifting gas*. This means that balloons filled with helium float upwards.

2 Helium is used in:
- party balloons
- weather balloons
- airships.

> Hydrogen is also much less dense than air. It was used in the past to fill airships, but hydrogen is flammable. The advantage of helium is that it is not flammable, reducing the risk of explosion.

Exam tip

PRACTICE QUESTIONS

1 Name three noble gases.

2 Why is helium used as a lifting gas?

3 Why is argon used in filament lamps?

4 Explain why there are no naturally occurring compounds of the noble gases..

THE BARE BONES

➤ Heat can be transferred by radiation, conduction and convection.

➤ Conduction and convection involve particles.

➤ All objects emit and absorb infra red radiation, but different surfaces are better at doing this than others.

A Thermal energy

1 Heat energy is also called thermal energy.

2 The atoms in solids, liquids and gases are always vibrating and moving. Their movements increase when they absorb thermal energy.

KEY FACT **3** Thermal energy can be transferred from place to place by *conduction*, *convection* and *radiation*.

B Conduction

KEY FACTS **1** Conduction of thermal energy needs *particles*.

2 Conduction works best in *solids* because their particles are close together. It cannot happen through empty space.

3 Thermal energy is transferred from the *hotter part* of an object to the colder part. The particles in the hot part are vibrating more. These vibrations are passed on to the cooler particles next to them. In this way, energy spreads through the substance.

4 Metals are good *heat conductors*.
Most non-metals, liquids and gases are poor heat conductors.

5 Insulators are poor conductors of heat. They keep things cold as well as hot. Air is a good insulator. Several layers of clothing will keep you warmer than one thick layer because the layers trap air between them.

C Convection

1 Convection of thermal energy needs *particles*.

2 Convection works in *liquids* and *gases* because their particles can move from place to place. It cannot happen in solids or empty space.

3 • When a liquid or gas warms up, it *expands* and becomes *less dense*.
 • The warmer liquid or gas *moves up* through the cooler liquid or gas.
 • It cools, contracts and becomes denser again, so it *sinks*.
 • This creates a *flow* called a convection current.

D Radiation

1 All objects *emit* (give off) and *absorb* (take in) thermal radiation. The hotter an object is, the more energy it emits.

2 Thermal energy can be transferred as infra red radiation, also called thermal radiation. Transfer of thermal energy by radiation does not need particles. It can happen through empty space.

3 Dark, dull (matt) surfaces are good emitters and absorbers of infra red radiation. Light, shiny surfaces are poor emitters and absorbers of infra red radiation.

E Factors affecting heat transfer

1 The *rate of transfer* of thermal energy depends on:
 • the *type* of material • the *shape* of the object • the *size* of the object
 • the *difference in temperature* between the object and its surroundings –
 the bigger the difference, the faster the rate of transfer.

PRACTICE QUESTIONS

1 Why can you feel thermal energy from the Sun, even though it is 150 million km away in space?

2 Explain why putting a lid on a cup of coffee keeps the coffee warmer for longer.

3 Suggest why satellites and spacecraft are often covered by sheets of shiny metal foil.

Efficiency

THE BARE BONES

➤ Energy is measured in joules, J.
➤ The efficiency of a device is the proportion of the energy usefully transformed by the device.

A Energy transfers and transformations

KEY FACTS

1 Energy is measured in joules, J.

2 Energy cannot be created or destroyed.

3 Energy can be *transferred* from place to place, or *transformed* from one type to another.

4 For example:
- Thermal energy is transferred from one place to another by infra red radiation.
- Electrical energy is transferred from the power station to our homes through cables.
- A battery transforms chemical energy into electrical energy.
- A filament lamp transforms electrical energy into light energy.

B Useful transfers and transformations

KEY FACTS

1 In any process or device, only some of the energy is *usefully transferred* or *transformed*. For example, a filament lamp transforms electrical energy into light energy, but it also transforms electrical energy into thermal energy.

2 The energy that is not usefully transferred or transformed is often called *wasted energy*.

Remember
Wasted energy is not destroyed.

B Useful transfers and transformations *cont.*

KEY FACT **3** Energy that is transferred or transformed is eventually *transferred to the surroundings as thermal energy.* The surroundings warm up as a result. But the energy spreads out so much that it becomes very difficult to do anything useful with it.

device	useful energy transformation	main energy wastage
filament lamp	electrical → light	electrical → thermal
car engine	chemical → kinetic	chemical → thermal chemical → sound

You should be able to identify the main energy wastages in different devices.

C Efficiency

KEY FACT **1** The efficiency of a device tells you what percentage of the energy used by the device is usefully transferred or transformed. It is calculated using this equation:

$$\text{efficiency} = \frac{\text{useful energy transferred by device}}{\text{total energy supplied to device}}$$

2 An ordinary filament lamp may transform 100 J of electrical energy to 10 J of light energy. The rest is transformed to thermal energy. Its efficiency is:

$$\text{efficiency} = \frac{\text{useful energy transferred by device}}{\text{total energy supplied to device}} = \frac{10}{100} = 0.1$$

An 'energy efficient' lamp may transform 100 J of electrical energy to 75 J of light energy. Its efficiency is 0.75 – it wastes much less energy as thermal energy.

> **Exam tip**
> If you calculate efficiency and it is 1.0 or more, you have gone wrong. Efficiency is always less than 1.0 because some energy is wasted.

PRACTICE QUESTIONS

1 What is 'wasted' energy?

2 What happens when energy is eventually transferred to the surroundings?

3 The efficiency of a coal-fired power station is 0.35 – how much electrical energy is produced from coal containing 100 MJ of chemical energy?

4 A television set transfers 200 J of electrical energy as 140 J of sound and light energy. What is its efficiency?

Cost of electricity

THE BARE BONES

➤ The power of a device is the rate at which it transforms energy.

➤ Power is measured in watts, W, or kilowatts, kW.

➤ The total cost of the electricity used by a device depends upon its power, how long it is run for, and the cost of a unit of electricity.

A Energy and power

KEY FACTS

1 The power of a device is the rate at which it transforms energy. The greater the power of a device, the more energy it transfers every second.

2 Power is measured in watts, W.
It can also be measured in kilowatts, kW.

Remember
1 kW = 1000 W.
To convert from W to kW, divide by 1000.

3 A 2 kW electric kettle transforms energy at a greater rate than a 100 W electric lamp.

B Electrical energy transferred from the mains

KEY FACTS

1 The *electrical energy transferred* from the mains supply depends on:

• the power of the device, and

• how long it is switched on.

2 Energy is normally measured in joules, J.
For mains electricity, electrical energy is measured in kilowatt-hours, kWh.

3 The electrical energy transferred is calculated using this equation:

energy transferred   =   power   ×   time
kilowatt-hours, kWh   kilowatt, kW   hour, h

4 Example A 2 kW electric kettle is switched on for 3 minutes.
How much energy is transferred?

Answer Convert minutes to hours by dividing by 60:
3 minutes = 3 ÷ 60 = 0.05 h
energy transferred = power × time = 2 × 0.05 = 0.1 kWh

5 Example A 100 W electric lamp is switched on for 2 hours.
How much energy is transferred?

Answer Convert W to kW by dividing by 1000:
100 W = 100 ÷ 1000 = 0.1 kW
energy transferred = power × time = 0.1 × 2 = 0.2 kWh
Notice that the lamp used twice as much electrical
energy as the kettle in these examples.

Remember
1 hour = 60 minutes.
To convert from minutes to
hours, divide by 60.

C Cost of electrical energy from the mains

FACT **1** The *cost of electrical energy transferred* from the mains supply depends on:
- the energy used by the device, and
- the cost of a unit of electrical energy.

2 1 kWh is 1 *unit* of electrical energy.

Y FACT **3** The cost of electrical energy transferred is calculated using this equation:

total cost = number of kilowatt-hours × cost per kilowatt-hour

4 Example An electric fire uses 2 kWh of electrical energy.
If 1 kWh costs 10p, how much does the fire cost to run per hour?

Answer total cost = number of kilowatt-hours × cost per kilowatt-hour
total cost = 2 × 10 = *20p*

PRACTICE QUESTIONS

1 What is the unit of power?

2 Write the equation that links electrical energy transferred from the mains with power and time.

3 How much electrical energy is transferred when a 250 W television set is used for 8 hours?

4 A 100 W electric lamp is switched on for 6 hours. If 1 kWh costs 10p, how much did the lamp cost to run?

THE BARE BONES

➤ The National Grid transfers electricity from power stations to consumers.
➤ Step-up transformers increase the voltage, and step-down transformers reduce it.
➤ Transformers are used in the National Grid to reduce energy losses in the cables.

A The National Grid

KEY FACT **1** The National Grid transfers electricity from power stations to consumers.

2 The National Grid consists of many electrical cables, some underground and some overground, suspended from pylons. It is designed so that it can still supply electricity when demand increases suddenly, or a power station fails.

3 Power stations produce electricity at 25 000 V. Electricity is sent through the National Grid cables at 400 000 V, 275 000 V and 132 000 V. These high voltages are needed to reduce energy losses during transmission.

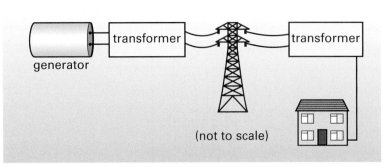

generator — transformer — (not to scale) — transformer

There are many ways to generate electricity, including nuclear power and wind power.

Exam tip

You don't have to remember these voltages, but you do need to know why high voltages are used.

B Energy losses

1 For a given rate of electrical energy transfer, the *higher the voltage* the *lower the current*.

2 Cables heat up when electricity is passed through them. When thermal energy is transferred from cables, energy is wasted. These losses must be reduced.

KEY FACT **3** The National Grid uses *high voltages* so that the *current is reduced*. This reduces the *energy losses* from the cables.

C Transformers

1 A transformer is an electrical device that *changes the voltage* of an alternating current, such as the mains electricity supply.

2 There are two main types of transformer:
- step-up transformers increase the voltage
- step-down transformers decrease the voltage.

3 The *high voltages* used by the National Grid reduce energy losses, but they are *too dangerous* to use in homes.

KEY FACTS **4** *Step-up transformers* increase the voltage from power stations so that energy losses from the cables are reduced.

5 *Step-down transformers* reduce the voltage from the cables to safer levels for supply to homes.

Remember

The voltage of household electricity is about 230V, but this is still dangerous.

PRACTICE QUESTIONS

1 What is the National Grid?

2 Explain why electricity is transferred from power stations to consumers at high voltages.

3 Describe how transformers are used in the National Grid.

THE BARE BONES

➤ Electricity is generated in power stations.

➤ Most electricity is generated from fossil fuels or nuclear fuels.

➤ An energy source is used to produce steam from water, which is used to drive a turbine coupled to a generator.

A Energy sources

1 Most power stations use *fossil fuels* or *nuclear fuels*.

KEY FACTS **2** *Thermal energy* is released from the fuel and used to *heat water*.

3 Steam from the boiling water expands and pushes against the blades of a turbine.

4 The turbine is connected to a generator. When the turbine spins, it turns the generator and electricity is produced.

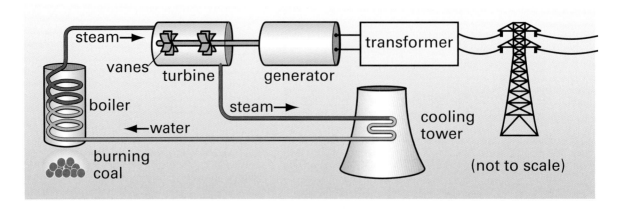

1 There are several energy transfers involved in generating electricity from fossil fuels or nuclear fuels. Energy is wasted at each step. The efficiency of a coal-fired power station is about 37%, and the efficiency of a nuclear power station is about 42%.

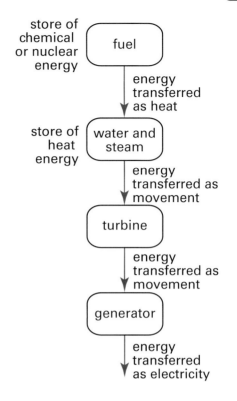

store of chemical or nuclear energy → fuel

energy transferred as heat

store of heat energy → water and steam

energy transferred as movement

turbine

energy transferred as movement

generator

energy transferred as electricity

2 Power stations that use *fossil fuels* burn *coal*, *natural gas* or *oil* to produce thermal energy.

3 *Nuclear* power stations use *uranium* or *plutonium*. These radioactive metals produce thermal energy because of nuclear reactions in them. The type of nuclear reaction is called nuclear fission.

You don't need to know any details of nuclear reactions in GCSE Science. You will find out about them if you study GCSE Additional Science.

Exam tip

PRACTICE QUESTIONS

1 Name three fossil fuels and two nuclear fuels.
2 Explain how thermal energy is used to produce electricity in a power station.
3 Suggest why the efficiency of power stations is quite low.

THE BARE BONES

➤ Renewable energy sources include wind power, wave power, tidal power, hydroelectric power, solar power and geothermal energy.

➤ Electricity can be generated from renewable energy sources.

A Renewable energy sources

KEY FACTS **1** Renewable energy sources will not run out, as long as they are managed effectively.

2 Energy from wind, waves, tides and hydroelectric schemes can be used to drive turbines directly.

B Wind power

1 Wind turbines have huge blades mounted on a tall tower. The blades are connected to a generator. As the wind blows, it transfers some of its kinetic energy to the blades. These turn and drive the generator. *Wind farms* consist of several wind turbines grouped together in windy locations.

KEY FACTS **2** There are *no fuel costs* for a wind turbine and *no polluting gases* are produced.

3 Wind farms are *noisy* and may spoil the view. If there is no wind, no electricity is generated.

C Water power

1 *Waves* at sea make the water level rise and fall. Wave machines use the kinetic energy in this movement to drive generators.

2 The *tides* cause huge amounts of water to move in and out of a river estuary each day. A tidal barrage is a barrier built across a river estuary. It contains electricity generators, which are driven by water moving through pipes in the barrage as the tide changes.

3 Hydroelectric power schemes use the kinetic energy in moving water. A *dam* is built across a river valley. The water high up behind the dam contains gravitational potential energy. This is transferred to kinetic energy as the water moves down through pipes inside the dam. The moving water drives electricity generators.

EY FACTS **4** Tidal barrages and hydroelectric power stations are very *reliable*. They can be turned on quickly.

5 Tidal barrages destroy the habitat of estuary species, such as wading birds. Dams flood farmland and people lose their homes. Rotting vegetation underwater releases methane, which is a greenhouse gas.

D Solar power

EY FACTS **1** Solar cells convert light energy directly into electrical energy.

2 Solar cells are convenient for supplying electricity to small portable devices such as calculators, or to devices in remote areas such as road signs.

3 Solar cells are expensive and inefficient, so the cost of their electricity is high. They do not work at night.

E Geothermal energy

EY FACTS **1** Geothermal energy is thermal energy in hot rocks deep underground.

2 In some *volcanic areas*, *hot water* or *steam* rises to the surface. In other places, cold water can be pumped down to the hot rocks, and returns as hot water. The heat energy is used to drive turbines connected to electricity generators.

PRACTICE QUESTIONS

1 Outline three ways that the energy in moving water can be used to generate electricity.
2 Suggest why solar cells are used to supply electricity to satellites.
3 Explain why geothermal energy is sometimes described as only partly renewable.

Resources compared

THE BARE BONES

➤ Fossil fuels, nuclear fuels and renewable energy sources have different advantages and disadvantages for generating electricity.
➤ Factors to take into account include building costs, start-up times, reliability, the relative cost of the electricity produced, and the place where it is needed.

A Building costs and fuel costs

KEY FACT **1** Different types of power station have different *building costs*. This affects the cost of the electricity produced during the lifetime of the power station.

2 In general, large and complex power stations cost the most to build. Nuclear power stations are very complex machines. They are very expensive to build but nuclear fuels are relatively cheap. Hydroelectric power schemes and tidal barrages are expensive but do not need any fuel.

3 Gas and oil are expensive fuels compared to coal. Wind turbines and solar cells do not need any fuel.

B Start-up times

KEY FACT **1** Different types of power station have different *start-up times*. This affects the way in which the power station is used.

2 Hydroelectricity stations can be started almost immediately.
Wind turbines start to work as soon as the wind reaches a certain speed.
Solar cells produce electricity as long as light falls on them.

type of power station	start-up time
gas-fired	shortest
oil-fired	
coal-fired	
nuclear	longest

The main types of power stations have different start-up times.

1 Some types of power station are more *reliable* than others.

2 Tidal barrages are reliable. They generate electricity as the tide comes in, and this happens twice a day. Some designs also work as the tide goes out.

3 Hydroelectric power stations are reliable. Their dams store water so that electricity can be generated all year round, and not just when a river is flowing quickly.

4 Wind turbines and solar cells are less reliable. Wind turbines only work when it is windy, and solar cells only work during the day.

> **Exam tip**
>
> Be prepared to use information in the exam to discuss the advantages and disadvantages of using different energy sources to generate electricity.

PRACTICE QUESTIONS

1 Extra electricity is needed at peak times of the day. Suggest why oil-fired and gas-fired power stations usually provide this electricity.

2 'Base load electricity' is generated all the time, whatever the demand on the National Grid. Suggest why nuclear power stations and coal-fired power stations usually provide this electricity.

3 Explain why electricity is supplied to the National Grid from many different types of power station, rather than just one type.

THE BARE BONES

➤ Electromagnetic radiation travels as waves.
➤ Waves can be described by their wave speed, frequency and wavelength.
➤ The electromagnetic spectrum can be grouped into different types, such as visible light and radio waves.
➤ All types of electromagnetic radiation travel at the same speed in space.

A Waves

1 Waves along a rope, water waves and light waves are all examples of *transverse waves*. The vibrations are at right angles to the direction of travel.

2 The amplitude of a wave is its maximum disturbance from its undisturbed position.

Remember
Take care: amplitude is not the distance between the top and bottom of a wave.

KEY FACTS **3** Waves move energy from one place to another.

4 The wavelength of a wave is the distance between a point on one wave and the same point on the next wave. The wavelength is measured in metres, m.

5 The frequency of a wave is the number of waves that pass a certain point each second. Frequency is measured in hertz, Hz. 1 Hz is one wave per second.

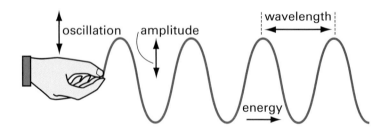

It is often easiest to measure the wavelength from the top of one wave to the top of the next wave.

Exam tip

KEY FACT **1** Electromagnetic waves can be described by this equation:

wave speed	=	frequency	×	wavelength
metre/second, m/s		hertz, Hz		metre, m

2 All electromagnetic waves travel at the same speed in a vacuum, such as space. This is extremely fast, about 300 000 000 m/s, but you don't need to remember the number.

3 **Example** A radio station broadcasts at 100 MHz (100 000 000 Hz). What is the wavelength of its radio waves?

Answer Re-arrange the equation:
wavelength = wave speed ÷ frequency
wavelength = 300 000 000 ÷ 100 000 000 = *3 m*

C The electromagnetic spectrum

KEY FACTS **1** The electromagnetic spectrum is a continuous range of waves, from waves with a very short wavelength to those with a very long wavelength.

2 Gamma rays have the shortest and radio waves have the longest wavelengths.

3 The longer the wavelength, the lower the frequency. So gamma rays have the highest frequency and radio waves have the lowest frequency.

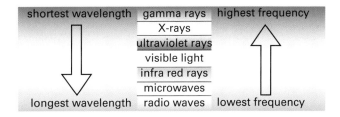

shortest wavelength — gamma rays — highest frequency
X-rays
ultraviolet rays
visible light
infra red rays
microwaves
longest wavelength — radio waves — lowest frequency

Make sure you know the order of the different types of radiation in the electromagnetic spectrum.

Exam tip

PRACTICE QUESTIONS

1 Write the equation that links wave speed, frequency and wavelength.

2 A wireless computer network operates at 2.4 GHz (2 400 000 000 Hz). If the wavelength is 0.125 m, calculate the wave speed.

3 Which type of electromagnetic radiation has the higher frequency, ultraviolet rays or infra red rays?

Some uses of electromagnetic radiation

THE BARE BONES

➤ The different types of electromagnetic radiation are absorbed, reflected or transmitted differently.

➤ The different types of electromagnetic radiation are used in different ways, depending on their properties.

A Gamma radiation

1 Gamma radiation cannot be seen or felt. It mostly passes through skin and soft tissue, but some of it is absorbed by cells.

2 Gamma radiation is used to:

- kill cancer cells

- kill harmful bacteria in food

- sterilise surgical instruments.

B X-rays

1 X-rays cannot be seen or felt. They mostly pass through skin and soft tissue, but they do not easily pass through bone or metal.

2 X-rays are used to:

- produce photographs of bones to check for damage such as fractures

- check metal components and welds for cracks or other damage.

C Ultraviolet radiation

1 We cannot see or feel ultraviolet radiation, but our skin responds to it by turning darker.

2 Ultraviolet radiation is used in:

- sun beds

- security pens

- fluorescent lights.

D   Infra red radiation

1 Infra red radiation is absorbed by the skin and we feel it as heat.

2 Infra red radiation is used in:

- night vision cameras
- television remote controls
- heaters, grills and toasters
- optical fibre communications.

Remember
Thermal energy is transferred through empty space by infra red radiation.

E   Microwaves and radio waves

1 Microwaves with certain wavelengths are absorbed by water molecules and can be used for cooking:

- water, fats and sugars easily absorb microwaves
- their molecules vibrate more vigorously, making the food in the oven hot.

2 Microwave radiation is also used in mobile phone and satellite communications.

3 Radio waves are used to transmit television and radio programmes.

> Microwaves and radio waves are absorbed by metal antennae, creating an alternating electrical current with the same frequency as the radiation.

Exam tip

PRACTICE QUESTIONS

1 How do our bodies detect infra red radiation if we cannot see it?

2 Outline how a microwave oven works.

3 Explain why X-rays can be used to check machinery for cracks without taking it apart.

THE BARE BONES

> ➤ Digital signals have advantages over analogue signals.
> ➤ Electromagnetic radiation can be used for communication.
> ➤ Visible light and infra red rays travel through optical fibres.
> ➤ Microwaves are used for satellite communications and mobile phones.

A Signals

KEY FACTS **1** Communication signals may be analogue or digital.

2 Analogue signals vary continuously.

The shape of an analogue signal matches the original wave.

3 Digital signals usually only have two values, 0 or 1.
This means that they are more easily processed by computers.

4 Signals become weaker as they travel. They also pick up random extra signals called *noise*. Noise causes hiss on radio programmes, and it causes internet connections to slow down as the modem tries to compensate.

KEY FACT **5** Digital signals are less affected by noise than analogue signals.

B Optical fibres

1 An optical fibre is a thin strand of glass with a protective coating. Light repeatedly reflects off the fibre's inner surface. In this way, light going in at one end emerges at the other end, even when the fibre is bent.

Y FACT **2** Infra red rays and visible light are used to send signals through optical fibres.

3 An optical fibre carries more information, and over greater distances, than an ordinary cable of the same thickness.

Light can follow a curved path through an optical fibre.

Remember to use a pencil and ruler to draw light rays.
Add one arrowhead for each ray.

Exam tip

C Radio waves and microwaves

1 Radio waves are used to transmit television and radio programmes. Long wavelength radio waves are reflected by the upper atmosphere. This lets them reach receivers over the horizon.

Y FACT **2** Microwaves are used to send information to and from satellites, and in mobile phone networks.

Microwaves pass straight through the Earth's atmosphere.

People are advised to keep their exposure to microwaves from mobile phones to a minimum.

PRACTICE QUESTIONS

1 Outline the differences between analogue signals and digital signals.
2 Explain why light can travel from one end to the other through an optical fibre.
3 Why are microwaves used to transmit information to and from satellites?

THE BARE BONES

➤ Electromagnetic radiation can affect living cells.
➤ The effects on cells depend on the type and amount of electro-magnetic radiation.

A Absorption of electromagnetic radiation

1 Exposure to very bright visible light can damage our eyesight. People who work with bright light, especially laser light, need to wear eye protection.

KEY FACTS **2** Some types of electromagnetic radiation mostly pass through soft tissue, such as skin and muscle, without being absorbed.

3 Some types of electromagnetic radiation are absorbed by soft tissue. This can cause:

- the tissue to heat up
- cells to become cancerous, or
- death of cells.

> **Exam tip**
> You need to be able to evaluate the possible hazards of using a particular type of electromagnetic radiation.

4 The particular effects on cells depend on the type and amount of electromagnetic radiation. For a given amplitude, high frequency radiation transfers more energy than low frequency radiation.

B Gamma radiation and X-rays

1 Gamma radiation and X-rays are very penetrating. *Exposure* to these types of electromagnetic radiation *increases the risk of cancer.*

2 Lead absorbs gamma radiation and X-rays. People who work with these types of radiation can minimise their exposure using *lead shielding.* For example, hospital radiographers may *leave the room* or stand behind a lead screen. They and their patients may wear lead aprons.

3 Radiotherapy treatment for cancer may use several weak beams of gamma radiation or X-rays that focus on the tumour. This way, healthy cells do not receive too much radiation and the tumour cells receive enough to kill them.

C Ultraviolet light

1 Ultraviolet radiation is found naturally in *sunlight*. It causes skin cancer.

2 *Our skin* responds to exposure to ultraviolet light by *turning darker*. This reduces the amount that reaches deeper skin tissues.

3 Exposure to ultraviolet light can be reduced by *avoiding the sun* and by using *sunscreen*.

D Microwaves

1 Microwave ovens are designed to prevent the user being exposed to microwave radiation. Safety features include:
- a *metal mesh* in the door to prevent microwaves escaping
- a *safety lock* that stops the oven working if the door is open.

2 There is concern that exposure to microwave radiation from *mobile phones* may be harmful, but the scientific evidence is not conclusive.

3 All mobile phones sold in the UK must produce SARs (Specific Absorption Rates) below a certain level. Users are advised to *reduce call times* and *increase the distance* of the phone from the head, for example by using a hands-free kit.

> You may be asked to evaluate information you are given about different ways to reduce exposure to electromagnetic radiation.
>
> **Exam tip**

PRACTICE QUESTIONS

1 Explain why a hospital radiographer may wear a lead apron.

2 Suggest why people are advised to wear hats and finely woven, loose fitting clothes when they go outside in the summer.

3 Describe two ways in which exposure to radiation from microwave ovens is prevented.

THE BARE BONES

➤ Isotopes are atoms of an element with the same number of protons but different numbers of neutrons.

➤ Radioactive substances give out radiation from the nuclei of their atoms.

A Atoms and isotopes

KEY FACTS **1** Atoms have a small central nucleus made of particles called protons and neutrons. Even smaller particles called electrons surround the nucleus.

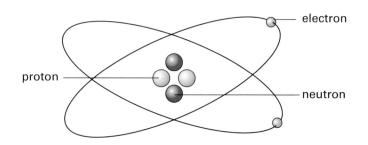

2 Atoms of an element all have the same number of protons.
Atoms of different elements have different numbers of protons.

3 Isotopes are atoms of an element that have the *same number of protons* but a *different number of neutrons*.
For example, carbon-12 and carbon-14 are isotopes of carbon.
Their atoms have six protons, but carbon-12 atoms have six neutrons and carbon-14 atoms have eight neutrons.

4 Some isotopes are radioactive. They are often called *radioisotopes*.

B Radioactivity

1 Atomic radiation consists of particles or electromagnetic waves given off by the nuclei of atoms.

KEY FACTS **2** Substances that give off radiation are radioactive.

3 Radioactive substances *give off radiation all the time*, whatever is done to them. Chemical reactions, heating or cooling have no effect on the radiation.

1 There are three main types of atomic radiation.

Alpha radiation consists of high energy particles from the nucleus. Each *alpha particle* is made from two protons and two neutrons, joined together.

Beta radiation also consists of high energy particles from the nucleus. Each *beta particle* is an electron, formed when a neutron breaks down.

Gamma radiation is high energy electromagnetic radiation from the nucleus.

2 They are called ionising radiation. This is because, when they collide with an atom, they can knock an electron out of the atom. The atom becomes an electrically charged particle called an ion.

D Properties of radiation

1 *Alpha radiation* and *beta radiation* are *deflected* from moving in straight lines by *electric fields* and *magnetic fields*. Gamma radiation is not affected.

2 *Alpha radiation* is the most ionising type of radiation and *gamma radiation* is the least ionising type.

radiation	distance travelled in air	stopped by		
		paper	thin aluminium	thick lead
alpha radiation	a few cm	✔	✔	✔
beta radiation	a few tens of cm		✔	✔
gamma radiation	many metres			✔

PRACTICE QUESTIONS

1 What are isotopes?
2 What types of radiation consists of particles?
3 Outline two differences in the properties of alpha, beta and gamma radiation.

Half-life

THE BARE BONES

➤ Radioactive substances give off less radiation as time goes by.

➤ Half-life is how long it takes for the number of nuclei of a radioactive isotope in a sample to halve.

➤ Different radioactive isotopes have different uses depending on factors such as their penetrating power, their ionising power, and their half-life.

A Half-life

1 Radioactive nuclei are *unstable*. They may decay at any time, releasing radiation. This *radioactive decay* helps the nucleus to become *more stable*.

KEY FACTS **2** Radioactive decay is a *random process*. You cannot predict when any individual nucleus will decay. But you can say that, after a certain amount of time, half the nuclei in a sample of the material will have decayed. This is the idea behind half–life.

3 The half-life of a radioactive isotope is defined as:

- the time taken for half the nuclei of that isotope in a sample to decay, or

- the time taken for the count rate from a sample to fall to half the starting rate.

4 Different radioactive isotopes have different half-lives. They vary from fractions of a second to millions of years.

Remember
The shape of the graph will be the same for all radioactive isotopes, it is just the axis labels that will change.

Technetium-99 is a gamma emitter. The graph shows how a sample of it decays. Technetium-99 has a half-life of six hours. So, if there is one gram at the start, after six hours this will have decayed to 0.5 g. After another six hours there will only be 0.25 g left.

The half–life will be the same wherever you measure it off the graph. Try to pick a sensible place on the graph.

Exam tip

KEY FACT

1 Some sources of radiation are better than others for particular jobs. When choosing the best one, take into account:

- the penetrating power
- the ionising power
- the half-life.

2 Alpha radiation does not travel very far, but it is very ionising. Sources of alpha radiation can damage living cells if swallowed. Gamma emitters are a better choice for *medical imaging*. Gamma radiation is the least ionising, and it will travel right out of the body to the detectors.

3 Radioactive tracers are used to follow chemicals in the environment or in the body. It is important that their half-life is long enough for the scientists or doctors to collect results, but not so long that they persist for a long time afterwards.

> Be prepared to analyse information about different radioactive isotopes to choose the best one for a particular job.
>
> **Exam tip**

PRACTICE QUESTIONS

1 State one definition of the term 'half-life'.

2 Iodine-125 has a half-life of 60 days. Starting with 8 g of iodine-125, how much will be left after 240 days?

3 Explain why technetium-99 is suitable for use in medical imaging.
Give two reasons in your answer.

THE BARE BONES

➤ Telescopes are used on Earth and in space to observe the universe.

➤ When a wave source moves towards or away from an observer, its observed wavelength and frequency changes.

➤ Light from distant galaxies is shifted towards the red end of the spectrum.

➤ Red-shift data provides evidence about the nature of the universe.

A Optical telescopes

1 Different types of telescope can observe the universe at different frequencies of electromagnetic radiation.

2 Optical telescopes are sensitive to visible light. Amateur astronomers use small telescopes, but very large ones are used by professional astronomers.

3 Ground-based optical telescopes can be used only at night and if the weather is good.

B Other telescopes

1 Objects in the universe do not just give off visible light. They also give off other electromagnetic radiation including radio waves, microwaves, X-rays and gamma rays.

2 Some telescopes can detect this radiation. They can be used in the daytime as well as at night, and they can be used in poor weather, because the radiation is not blocked by clouds.

3 Telescopes that detect X-rays and gamma rays produce very detailed images. This is because the wavelength of the electromagnetic radiation they detect is very small.

4 Space-based telescopes can be used all the time, but are very expensive and difficult to maintain.

> **Exam tip**
> Be prepared to use information in the exam to discuss the advantages and disadvantages of different types of telescope.

C The nature of the universe

1 Scientists have gathered a lot of evidence about the nature of the universe.

EY FACT **2** The accepted model of the universe is the **Big Bang theory**. It states that about 13.6 billion years ago all the matter in the universe was concentrated into a single very small point. This enlarged rapidly in a hot explosion. The universe is still expanding today.

D Red-shift

1 The wavelength and frequency of a source of waves changes if it moves towards or away from you. This is why the pitch of an ambulance siren rises and falls as it passes you.

EY FACTS **2** The light from galaxies is **red-shifted** because the observed wavelength of the light has increased. This is evidence that galaxies are moving away from us.

3 The further away the galaxy, the more its light is red-shifted. This means that the *more distant galaxies* are moving away *more quickly* than nearby ones.

4 This is evidence for the Big Bang: in an explosion, the fastest moving objects end up furthest away.

> You do not need to know the order of the planets for your exam. **Exam tip**

PRACTICE QUESTIONS

1 Give two advantages of radio telescopes over optical telescopes.
2 Outline the Big Bang theory of the origin of the universe.
3 Explain how red-shift evidence supports the Big Bang theory.

Unit B1a Human Biology

Specimen QUESTION ONE

This question is about white blood cells and how they help to defend the body against pathogens.

Match words, **A**, **B**, **C** and **D**, with the numbers **1 – 4** in the sentences.

A   antibodies
B   antigens
C   antitoxins
D   ingest

Pathogens have chemicals called ... **1** ... on their surface. White blood cells produce ... **2** ... and these stick to the pathogens.

White blood cells ... **3** ... pathogens and destroy them with reactive chemicals.

White blood cells also produce ... **4** ... that counteract toxins.

4 marks

Specimen QUESTION TWO

The diagram shows how nerve impulses travel in a reflex action.

Match words, **A**, **B**, **C** and **D**, with the numbers **1 – 4** on the flow chart.

A   effector
B   receptor
C   response
D   sensory neurone

4 marks

Specimen QUESTION THREE

The conditions in the body must be controlled.

Match words, **A**, **B**, **C** and **D**, with the numbers **1 – 4** in the sentences.

A   ions
B   lungs
C   sugar
D   urine

Water leaves the body from the ... **1** ... when we breathe out. Water and ... **2** ... leave the body from the kidneys in ... **3** ... The blood ... **4** ... level must be controlled to provide cells with a constant source of energy.

4 marks

Specimen QUESTION FOUR

This question is about tobacco smoke and alcohol, and the harm they can do to the body.

Match substances, **A**, **B**, **C** and **D**, with the features **1 – 4** in the table.

A   alcohol
B   carbon monoxide
C   nicotine
D   tar

	feature
1	the addictive substance in tobacco smoke
2	reduces the ability of red blood cells to carry oxygen
3	causes lung cancer
4	causes a lack of self control

4 marks

All the remaining questions have four parts.
Choose only one answer in each part, but you can use the same number more than once.

Specimen QUESTION FIVE

5A Which row in the table shows the correct source of each hormone?

	oestrogen	FSH	LH
1	ovaries	ovaries	pituitary
2	pituitary	ovaries	ovaries
3	ovaries	pituitary	ovaries
4	ovaries	pituitary	pituitary

5C Information passes across a synapse ...

1 by the diffusion of a chemical.

2 by nerve impulses crossing the gap.

3 by nerve impulses through a motor neurone.

4 by hormones produced by the pituitary.

5B Different hormones have different effects.

1 Oestrogen causes eggs to mature.

2 FSH causes eggs to mature.

3 FSH inhibits the production of oestrogen.

4 Oestrogen is useful as a fertility drug.

5D Your metabolic rate varies with the amount of activity you do.

1 The less exercise you take and the warmer it is, the less food you need.

2 The less exercise you take and the warmer it is, the more food you need.

3 The more exercise you take and the warmer it is, the more food you need.

4 The more exercise you take and the warmer it is, the less food you need.

4 marks

Unit B1a Human Biology *cont.*

Specimen QUESTION SIX

The graph shows the changes in the concentration of certain antibodies in the blood following vaccination.

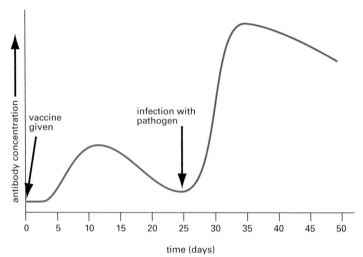

Graph of primary and secondary immune response.

6A How long after infection by the pathogen is the maximum antibody concentration reached?

1 10 days

2 12 days

3 25 days

4 37 days

6B Compared to the first immune response, the second immune response is ...

1 faster and larger.

2 faster and smaller.

3 slower and smaller.

4 slower and larger.

6C A vaccine may contain ...

1 a dead form of the disease.

2 an inactive form of the pathogen.

3 red blood cells that produce antibodies.

4 a mixture of antibiotics to kill pathogens.

6D The data on antibody concentration are presented as a line graph. This is because ...

1 the dependent variable is categoric and the independent variable is continuous.

2 the dependent variable is continuous and the independent variable is categoric.

3 both variables are categoric.

4 both variables are continuous.

4 marks

Answers Unit B1a

Question	A	B	C	D
ONE	2	1	4	3
TWO	3	1	4	2
THREE	2	1	4	3
FOUR	4	2	1	3
FIVE	4	2	1	1
SIX	1	1	2	4

Specimen QUESTION ONE

The question is about competition between living things.

Match words, **A**, **B**, **C** and **D**, with the numbers **1 – 4** in the sentences.

A	food
B	light
C	nutrients
D	territory

Animals defend their ... **1** ... and compete with each other for ... **2** ...

Plants compete with each other for ... **3** ... from the soil and ... **4** ...

4 marks

Specimen QUESTION TWO

The polar bear lives in the Arctic, where it is cold.
Polar bears have adaptations that let them survive in
the conditions found in the Arctic.

Match adaptations, **A**, **B**, **C** and **D**, with the numbers
1 – 4 in the table.

A	broad feet with claws
B	good sense of smell
C	thick layer of fat
D	white fur

	reason for adaptation
1	ice and snow is slippery
2	camouflage so prey cannot see them
3	to stay warm in the cold
4	to find prey for food

4 marks

Specimen QUESTION THREE

Human activities can affect the Earth's climate.

Match words, **A**, **B**, **C** and **D**, with the numbers **1 – 4** in the sentences.

A	carbon dioxide
B	fossil fuels
C	methane
D	thermal

Greenhouse gases absorb ... **1** ... energy radiated by the Earth.

The use of ... **2** ... increases the amount of ... **3** ... in the air.

Cattle and rice paddy fields increase the amount of ... **4** ... in the air.

4 marks

Unit B1b Evolution and Environment *cont.*

Specimen QUESTION FOUR

This question is about the cloning of animals.

Match words, **A**, **B**, **C** and **D**, with the numbers **1 – 4** in the sentences.

A   embryo
B   fusion
C   unfertilised egg
D   womb

The nucleus of an ... **1** ... cell is removed.

The nucleus from an ... **2** ... cell is then injected into the cell without a nucleus.

The egg cell is implanted into the ... **3** ... of a host mother, where it develops.

This is called ... **4** ... cell cloning.

4 marks

> All the remaining questions have four parts.
> Choose only one answer in each part, but you can use the same number more than once.

Specimen QUESTION FIVE

The theory of evolution explains how the different species of living things arose on Earth.

5A One reason why Darwin's theory of evolution by natural selection was only gradually accepted by most scientists was that ...

1 Darwin had no evidence.

2 Lamarck's theory of evolution was more accurate.

3 Darwin's theory conflicted with religious views.

4 most scientists refused to analyse Darwin's theory.

5B The dinosaurs became extinct millions of years ago. Which is the least likely reason for this?

1 New competitors evolved.

2 New predators evolved.

3 The climate changed.

4 People hunted them.

5C New forms of genes can appear because of ...

1 variation between individuals in a species.

2 sexual reproduction.

3 mutation.

4 cloning.

5D The theory of evolution states that all species of living things have evolved from simple life-forms which first developed about ...

1 three thousand years ago.

2 three million years ago.

3 three hundred million years ago.

4 three billion years ago.

4 marks

Specimen QUESTION SIX

Reducing the area of forest is called deforestation. The graph shows the amount of deforestation in the Amazon each year between 1988 and 2007.

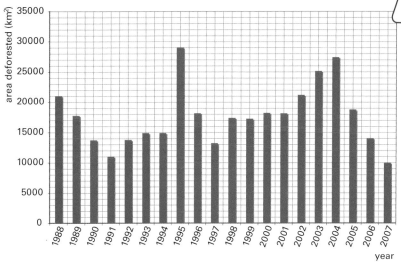

6A The data are presented as a bar chart. This is because ...

1 the dependent variable is categoric and the independent variable is continuous.

2 the dependent variable is continuous and the independent variable is categoric.

3 both variables are categoric.

4 both variables are continuous.

6B The mean amount of deforestation each year is about ...

1 $10\,000\,km^2$

2 $12\,500\,km^2$

3 $17\,500\,km^2$

4 $29\,000\,km^2$

6C Which statement is a valid conclusion from these data?

1 Deforestation is caused by human activity.

2 Deforestation is caused by natural events.

3 The amount of deforestation is almost the same each year.

4 The area of forest in the Amazon decreased in each year of the study.

6D Scientists were interested to see why deforestation was particularly high in 1995. The best way to gather evidence about this would be to ...

1 analyse satellite photographs of the Amazon taken in 1994 and 1995.

2 analyse data from 2004, as deforestation was also high then.

3 interview some local people for their ideas about the forest.

4 send scientists to all the deforested areas.

(4 marks)

Answers Unit B1b

Question	A	B	C	D
ONE	2	4	3	1
TWO	1	4	3	2
THREE	3	2	4	1
FOUR	2	4	1	3
FIVE	3	4	3	4
SIX	2	3	4	1

Unit C1a Products from Rocks

Specimen QUESTION ONE

This question is about atoms.

Match words, **A**, **B**, **C** and **D**, with the numbers **1 – 4** in the sentences.

A　　　bonds
B　　　electrons
C　　　element
D　　　nucleus

Atoms have a central ... **1** ... surrounded by ... **2** ... A substance made from one sort of atom is called an ... **3** ... The atoms in a compound are held together by chemical ... **4** ...

4 marks

Specimen QUESTION TWO

Limestone is a useful material.

The flow chart shows how some of its products are made.

Match adaptations, **A**, **B**, **C** and **D**, with the numbers **1 – 4** in the flow chart.

A　　　carbon dioxide
B　　　slaked lime
C　　　heat in a kiln
D　　　add water

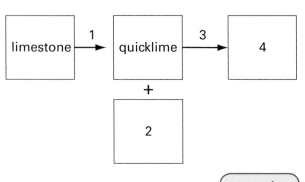

4 marks

Specimen QUESTION THREE

Natural gas and many other hydrocarbons are useful as fuels.
They produce many substances when they burn.

Match the substances, **A**, **B**, **C** and **D**, with the numbers **1 – 4** in the table.

A　　　carbon dioxide
B　　　natural gas
C　　　soot
D　　　sulfur dioxide

	what we can say about the substance
1	causes global warming
2	causes global dimming
3	causes acid rain
4	contains carbon and hydrogen

4 marks

Specimen QUESTION FOUR

This question is about metals and how they are extracted.

Match words, **A**, **B**, **C** and **D**, with the numbers **1 – 4** in the table.

A   copper
B   gold
C   iron
D   titanium

	what we can say about the metal
1	It is usually converted into steel.
2	It is expensive to extract because a lot of energy is needed.
3	It has properties that make it useful for electrical wires and plumbing.
4	It is an unreactive metal that can be found in the ground in its native state.

4 marks

> All the remaining questions have four parts.
> Choose only one answer in each part, but you can use the same number more than once.

Specimen QUESTION FIVE

Crude oil can be separated into fractions using fractional distillation.

5A Fractional distillation separates the hydrocarbons in crude oil according to their ...

1 density.
2 colour.
3 boiling point.
4 chemical reactivity.

5B Which statement is correct?

1 The fraction with the lowest boiling point and lowest viscosity is found at the top of the column.
2 The fraction with the highest boiling point and lowest viscosity is found at the top of the column.
3 The fraction with the highest boiling point and highest viscosity is found at the top of the column.
4 The fraction with the lowest boiling point and highest viscosity is found at the top of the column.

5C The chemical formula of ethane is C_2H_6 and the formula of propane is C_3H_8. The formula of pentane is:

1 C_5H_8
2 C_5H_{10}
3 C_5H_{12}
4 C_5H_{14}

5D Methane burns completely in air to produce carbon dioxide and water vapour. The correct equation for this reaction is:

1 $CH_4 + O_2 \rightarrow CO_2 + 2H_2O$
2 $CH_4 + 2O_2 \rightarrow CO_2 + 2H_2O$
3 $CH_4 + O_2 \rightarrow CO + 2H_2O$
4 $CH_4 + 2O_2 \rightarrow 2CO + 2H_2O$

4 marks

Unit C1a Products from Rocks *cont.*

Specimen QUESTION SIX

Read the information in the box about recycling aluminium.

> It takes 14 kWh of electricity to make 1 kg of aluminium from aluminium ore. Making aluminium by recycling uses just 5% of the electricity needed to make aluminium from aluminium ore. Every time 1 kg of aluminium is recycled, 8 kg of aluminium ore is saved and 4 kg of waste is not produced.

6A The amount of electricity saved by recycling 1 kg of aluminium is:

1 0.7 kWh

2 7 kWh

3 13.3 kWh

4 13.5 kWh

6B An aluminium can weighs about 15 g. How much waste is saved by recycling 80 cans, the average number used by each person in the UK each year?

1 60 g

2 320 g

3 1200 g

4 4800 g

6C Recycling aluminium uses less electricity than making aluminium from aluminium oxide because …

1 the aluminium oxide has aleady been reduced.

2 most aluminium is mixed with other metals to make alloys.

3 aluminium has a low density and resists corrosion.

4 aluminium is a transition metal.

6D Aluminium is more expensive to produce than iron. This is because …

1 there is more iron ore in the Earth's crust than aluminium ore.

2 iron is more reactive than aluminium.

3 iron can be produced by reaction with carbon, but aluminium cannot.

4 pure iron is very soft.

(4 marks)

Answers Unit C1a

Question	A	B	C	D
ONE	4	2	3	1
TWO	2	4	1	3
THREE	1	4	2	3
FOUR	3	4	1	2

Specimen QUESTION ONE

The atmospheres of Mars and Earth are mixtures of gases.

Match gases, **A**, **B**, **C** and **D**, with the numbers **1 – 4** in the table.

A   carbon dioxide
B   helium
C   nitrogen
D   oxygen

	what we can say about the gas
1	It is the main gas in the atmosphere of Mars.
2	It is produced by photosynthesis in plants.
3	It is the main gas in the Earth's atmosphere.
4	It is one of the noble gases.

4 marks

Specimen QUESTION TWO

This question is about the Earth's tectonic plates.

Match words, **A**, **B**, **C** and **D**, with the numbers **1 – 4** in the sentences.

A   convection
B   crust
C   heat
D   mantle

The Earth's ... **1** ... and upper part of the ... **2** ... are cracked into large pieces called tectonic plates.

The plates move because of ... **3** ... currents driven by ... **4** ... from natural radioactive processes inside the Earth.

4 marks

Specimen QUESTION THREE

Hydrocarbon molecules in oil fractions can be cracked at the oil refinery.

Match words, **A**, **B**, **C** and **D**, with the numbers **1 – 4** in the flow chart.

A   hydrocarbons are heated
B   small hydrocarbon molecules
C   large hydrocarbon molecules
D   vapours are passed over a hot catalyst

4 marks

Unit C1b Oils, Earth and Atmosphere *cont.*

Specimen QUESTION FOUR

This question is about vegetable oils and their reactions.

Match words, **A**, **B**, **C** and **D**, with the numbers **1 – 4** in the sentences.

A   emulsions
B   nickel
C   iodine
D   hydrogen

The presence of double carbon–carbon bonds can be detected because of a colour change when ... **1** ... is mixed with vegetable oils.

Unsaturated oils can be hardened to make them suitable for cakes and margarine by reacting them with ... **2** ... at about 60 °C with a catalyst of ... **3** ...

Vegetable oils form ... **4** ... when shaken with water.

4 marks

> All the remaining questions have four parts.
> Choose only one answer in each part, but you can use the same number more than once.

Specimen QUESTION FIVE

Hydrocarbons called alkenes are produced by cracking.

5A What is the general formula for an alkene?

1 C_nH_{2n+2}

2 C_nH_{n+2}

3 $C_{2n}H_n$

4 C_nH_{2n}

5B Why are alkenes described as unsaturated?

1 They contain double carbon–carbon bonds.

2 They are hydrocarbons.

3 They contain single carbon–carbon bonds.

4 They react with oxygen.

5C The chemical formula of ethene is C_2H_4 and the formula of propene is C_3H_6. The formula of pentene is:

1 C_5H_8

2 C_5H_{10}

3 C_5H_{12}

4 C_5H_{14}

5D Ethanol is useful as a fuel. It can be produced by the fermentation of sugar, or by the reaction of ethene with steam. One advantage of producing ethanol by fermentation is that ...

1 it uses non-renewable resources.

2 sugar is a renewable resource.

3 it takes place in the presence of a catalyst.

4 ethanol is the only product of the reaction of ethene with steam.

4 marks

Specimen QUESTION SIX

Artificial colours in food can be detected and identified by chromatography.

The different substances can be identified by their R_f (retention factor) value:

$$R_f = \frac{\text{distance travelled by the substance}}{\text{distance travelled by the solvent}}$$

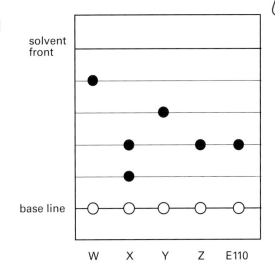

6A In the chromatogram, what is the R_f value of E110?

1 0.2

2 0.4

3 0.6

4 2.5

6B From the information in the chromatogram, what can be said about the substances W, X, Y and Z?

1 X and Z are the same substance.

2 X is a mixture of W and Z.

3 Z is found in X but not in Y.

4 Z is more soluble in the solvent than W.

6C E110 is also called sunset yellow. The chromatography results show that ...

1 Z must be yellow.

2 X and Z must contain E110.

3 Z could be sunset yellow.

4 X is likely to be orange coloured.

6D Food additives may be given E numbers to show that ...

1 they are artificial.

2 they could cause allergies in some people.

3 they improve the shelf life of the food.

4 they are permitted for use in food.

(**4 marks**)

Answers Unit C1b

Question	A	B	C	D
ONE	1	4	3	2
TWO	3	1	4	2
THREE	2	4	1	3
FOUR	4	3	1	2
FIVE	4	1	2	2
SIX	2	3	3	4

Unit P1a Energy and Electricity

Specimen QUESTION ONE

Televisions transform energy.

Match types of energy, **A**, **B**, **C** and **D**, with the numbers **1 – 4** in the sentences.

A	light
B	electrical
C	thermal
D	sound

The energy input to the television is ... **1** ... energy. The useful type of energy output by the screen is ... **2** ... energy. The useful type of energy output by the loudspeakers is ... **3** ... energy. The type of energy not usefully output by the television is ... **4** ... energy.

Specimen QUESTION TWO

The use of renewable energy resources to generate electricity reduces the need to use fossil fuels. This question is about advantages and disadvantages of renewable energy resources.

	feature
1	convenient for supplying electricity to small portable devices
2	farmland is flooded
3	may be seen from a long distance and so spoil the view
4	mostly only available in volcanic areas

Match the words, **A**, **B**, **C** and **D**, with the numbers **1 – 4** in the table.

A	geothermal energy stations
B	solar cells
C	wind farms
D	hydroelectric power schemes

4 marks

Specimen QUESTION THREE

The flow chart shows the main events in a conventional power station.

Match the words, **A**, **B**, **C** and **D**, with the numbers **1 – 4** in the sentences.

A	electrical
B	kinetic
C	steam
D	thermal

The burning fuel releases ... **1** ... energy.

The turbine spins because ... **2** ... pushes against it.

The turbine transfers ... **3** ... energy to the generator.

The generator produces ... **4** ... energy.

thermal energy released from fuel

water boils

turbine spins

generator turns

4 marks

Specimen QUESTION FOUR

A vacuum flask maintains the temperature of drinks longer than ordinary containers.

It has several features to help reduce the transfer of thermal energy to and from it.

Match features, **A**, **B**, **C** and **D**, with the reasons **1 – 4** in the table.

A   silvery walls
B   stopper on the flask
C   thin glass walls
D   vacuum between the glass walls

	reason
1	reduces heat losses from the top by convection
2	reduces heat losses from the sides by convection
3	reduces absorption and emission of infra red radiation
4	reduces heat losses through the wall by conduction

4 marks

All the remaining questions have four parts.
Choose only one answer in each part, but you can use the same number more than once.

Specimen QUESTION FIVE

Modern electrical appliances such as fridges and dishwashers are given 'efficiency ratings'.
G is the least efficient and A is the most efficient.

5A Compared to a G rated dishwasher, an A rated dishwasher ...

1 usefully transforms a bigger proportion of the electrical energy supplied to it.

2 usefully transforms a smaller proportion of the electrical energy supplied to it.

3 uses less water.

4 dries the dishes for you.

5B The power of a certain dishwasher is listed as 1250 W. This is the same as:

1 125 kW

2 12.5 kW

3 1.25 kW

4 0.125 kW

5C An electric light bulb releases 4 J of light energy when it is supplied with 16 J of electrical energy. What is its efficiency?

1 0.25

2 0.40

3 0.75

4 4.00

5D How much electrical energy, in kWh, is transferred when a 0.2 kW television set is used for 30 minutes?

1 0.1

2 2.5

3 6.0

4 150

4 marks

Unit P1a Energy and Electricity *cont.*

Specimen QUESTION SIX

Different energy resources can be used to generate electricity. Scientists and politicians must carefully consider the advantages and disadvantages of each energy resource. They must ensure that the UK continues to generate the electricity it needs, while minimising harm to the environment.

6A A typical wind turbine needs 1.2 million kWh of electricity in its manufacture. It generates 96 million kWh of electricity in its 20 year lifetime. How long is needed for the turbine to generate more electricity than was needed to make it?

1 3 months

2 4 months

3 3 years

4 6.7 years

6B Which of the following is a disadvantage of nuclear power stations?

1 They produce almost no greenhouse gases while in use.

2 They run continuously so they supply 'base load' electricity.

3 Nuclear waste is difficult to handle and store safely.

4 Nuclear fuels release heat in a nuclear reactor.

6C Which of the following are non-renewable energy resources?

1 natural gas and tidal power

2 oil and uranium

3 wind power and uranium

4 wave energy and coal

6D Which of the following energy resources does not ultimately rely on energy from the Sun?

1 solar power

2 hydroelectric power

3 wind power

4 tidal power

4 marks

Answers Unit P1a

Question	A	B	C	D
ONE	2	1	4	3
TWO	4	1	3	2
THREE	4	3	2	1
FOUR	3	1	4	2
FIVE	1	3	1	1
SIX	1	3	2	4

Specimen QUESTION ONE

Different types of electromagnetic radiation have different uses.

Match the types of electromagnetic radiation, **A**, **B**, **C** and **D**, with the numbers **1 – 4** in the table.

A   X-rays
B   infra red rays
C   microwaves
D   ultraviolet rays

	use
1	making medical images
2	mobile telephone communications
3	tanning beds
4	television remote controls

4 marks

Specimen QUESTION TWO

The different types of electromagnetic radiation can be put in order of decreasing frequency.

Match words, **A**, **B**, **C** and **D**, with the numbers **1 – 4** in the table.

A   infra red light
B   visible light
C   radio waves
D   X-rays

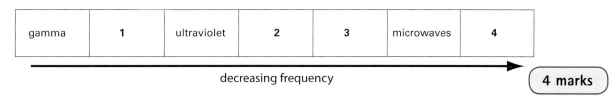

gamma	1	ultraviolet	2	3	microwaves	4

decreasing frequency

4 marks

Specimen QUESTION THREE

Electromagnetic radiation can harm us if it is used incorrectly.

Match words, **A**, **B**, **C** and **D**, with the numbers **1 – 4** in the sentences.

A   infra red radiation
B   X-rays
C   ultraviolet light
D   microwave radiation

Exposure to ... **1** ... can cause skin cancer.

Cells are damaged when ... **2** ... heats up the water inside them.

There is a risk from exposure to ... **3** ... of causing mutations in unborn babies.

... **4** ... is felt as heat and can cause burns.

4 marks

Unit P1b Radiation and the Universe *cont.*

Specimen QUESTION FOUR

Telescopes are used to observe the universe and to provide scientists with evidence about it.

Match words, **A, B, C** and **D**, with the numbers **1 – 4** in the sentences.

A   the universe
B   galaxies
C   point
D   Earth

Telescopes on ... **1** ... that detect radio waves can work all the time.

Light from distant ... **2** ... is red-shifted.

4 marks

The observed red-shift is evidence that ... **3** ... began as a very small ... **4** ... in a 'big bang'.

> All the remaining questions have four parts.
> Choose only one answer in each part, but you can use the same number more than once.

Specimen QUESTION FIVE

Radioactive materials give off radiation.

5A Which row in the table is correct?

	made of particles?		
	alpha	**beta**	**gamma**
1	✔	✗	✗
2	✔	✗	✔
3	✗	✔	✔
4	✔	✔	✗

5B Which row in the table is correct?

	deflected by an electric field?		
	alpha	**beta**	**gamma**
1	✔	✔	✗
2	✔	✗	✗
3	✔	✗	✔
4	✗	✔	✔

5C A computer WiFi wireless network operates at 2.4 GHz (2 400 000 000 Hz).
If the wavelength is 0.125 m, what is the wave speed of the WiFi signal in m/s?

1 19 200 000

2 300 000 000

3 3 000 000 000

4 19 200 000 000

5D WiFi networks use digital signals rather than analogue signals.
Which statement is correct?

1 Digital signals are less prone to interference than analogue signals.

2 Analogue signals are more easily processed by computers.

3 Digital signals are continuously varying.

4 Digital signals can travel through optical fibres but analogue signals cannot.

4 marks

Half-life is the time needed for the number of nuclei of a radioactive isotope in a sample, to halve. Carbon-14 has a half-life of 5730 years. It is taken up by living things while they are alive. Objects made from animal or plant materials can be dated by finding the amount of carbon-14 they still contain.

6A A sample of ancient cloth contains 4 million carbon-14 atoms. Which row in the table is correct?

	number of carbon-14 atoms in sample	
	5730 years ago	**in 5730 years time**
1	2 million	1 million
2	8 million	2 million
3	8 million	1 million
4	2 million	8 million

6B Beta radiation consist of ...

1 helium nuclei released from carbon-14 nuclei.

2 high frequency electromagnetic radiation.

3 high energy electrons surrounding carbon-14 nuclei.

4 high energy electrons released from carbon-14 nuclei.

6C One reason why carbon-14 is not suitable as a tracer for medical images is that ...

1 beta radiation is absorbed by the body before it reaches the detector.

2 beta radiation is the most ionising form of radiation.

3 only ancient materials contain carbon-14.

4 its half-life is too short.

6D Rocks may be millions of years old. One reason why carbon-14 is not suitable for dating rocks is that ...

1 rocks do not contain carbon.

2 it is difficult to prepare rock samples for dating.

3 beta radiation cannot escape from rocks.

4 the number of carbon-14 atoms in a rock would be too small to measure.

(4 marks)

Answers Unit P1b

Question	A	B	C	D
ONE	1	4	2	3
TWO	3	2	4	1
THREE	4	3	1	2
FOUR	3	2	4	1
FIVE	4	1	3	1
SIX	2	4	1	4

- Revise a group of topics, then have a go at these questions. Put a tick in the box if you know the answer and a cross if you don't. Check your answers at the bottom of each page.
- Try the questions again the next time you revise. Aim to get a column that is all ticks.

Biology Unit B1a   Human Biology

Controlling the body

1 What does a sensory neurone do?

2 What is the function of a synapse?

3 State three ways in which water can leave the body.

4 What is a hormone?

5 What does the hormone FSH do?

Diet and health

6 State one health problem caused by a lack of food.

7 Name three health problems linked to excess weight.

8 What are LDLs and what do they do?

Drugs

9 Name the addictive substance in tobacco smoke.

10 Outline the problems caused by thalidomide.

Pathogens and disease

11 What is a pathogen?

12 State three ways in which white blood cells defend against disease.

13 Why should we be careful not to over-use antibiotics?

14 What is a vaccine?

Answers

1 Carries information from a receptor.

2 It is the gap between two neurones and it allows signals to pass from one neurone to the next.

3 Through the skin, kidneys and lungs.

4 A chemical produced by a gland and transported by the blood to a target organ, where it causes a change.

5 It causes an egg to mature and it stimulates the release of oestrogen.

6 Becoming too thin, irregular periods, reduced resistance to infection.

7 Three from: heart disease, high blood pressure, arthritis, diabetes.

8 Low-density lipoproteins. They carry cholesterol from the liver to the body's cells.

9 Nicotine.

10 It caused birth defects. It cannot be given to pregnant women.

11 A micro-organism that causes disease.

12 Produce antitoxins, produce antibodies, ingest and destroy pathogens.

13 Antibiotic-resistant strains may develop because of natural selection.

14 A dead or inactive form of a pathogen, usually injected.

Adaptation and evolution

1 Name three things that plants compete with each other for. □ □ □

2 What can happen to a species if a new predator is introduced? □ □ □

3 Outline the main features of Darwin's theory of evolution. □ □ □

4 What information can the study of fossils give us? □ □ □

Reproduction

5 What is fertilisation? □ □ □

6 Outline the differences between sexual and asexual reproduction. □ □ □

7 Where are the chromosomes found, and why are they important? □ □ □

Cloning and genetic engineering

8 How could an amateur gardener clone a plant? □ □ □

9 Outline how an embryo transplant is carried out. □ □ □

10 What is the main difference between fusion cell cloning and adult cell cloning? □ □ □

Pollution and global warming

11 Explain why the amount of waste humans produce is increasing. □ □ □

12 Name a gas that causes acid rain. □ □ □

13 Explain why carbon dioxide and methane are greenhouse gases. □ □ □

14 Name two biological sources of methane. □ □ □

Answers

1 Three from: light, water, nutrients (*not* food), space.
2 The species could become extinct.
3 Individuals in a species show variation caused by differences in their genes. Individuals with features best suited to the environment are more likely to survive to reproduce and pass on their beneficial genes.
4 Information about the development of life on Earth.
5 The fusion of a male gamete with a female gamete.

6 Sexual reproduction needs two parents and gives rise to variation because genes are mixed. Asexual reproduction needs one parent and gives rise to clones because genes are not mixed.
7 The cell's nucleus. They carry the genes.
8 Take a cutting.
9 A developing embryo is split in two at an early stage, grown in the laboratory and then implanted into host mothers.
10 The nucleus in fusion cell cloning comes from an embryo, and from a body cell of an adult animal in adult cell cloning.

11 One of: increase in population, increase in standard of living.
12 Sulfur dioxide (allow nitrogen oxides or NOx).
13 They absorb thermal energy radiated from the Earth and stop it escaping into space.
14 Cattle and rice paddy fields (allow biogas from sewage).

Chemistry Unit C1a   Products from Rocks

Atoms, elements and compounds

1 Describe the basic structure of an atom. □□□

2 What is a column in the periodic table called? □□□

3 What happens to electrons when chemical bonds form? □□□

4 What does the formula HNO_3 tell you? □□□

Limestone

5 What is the main compound found in limestone? □□□

6 Write the word equation for the thermal decomposition of copper carbonate. □□□

7 State two major uses of limestone or its products. □□□

Metals and ores

8 Why are iron from the blast furnace and pure iron unsuitable for most uses? □□□

9 What is an alloy? □□□

10 Explain why titanium and aluminium are expensive to extract. □□□

Alkanes and fuels

11 What is a hydrocarbon? □□□

12 Outline how alkanes from crude oil are separated by fractional distillation. □□□

13 Name the products of complete combustion of alkanes. □□□

14 State a problem caused by carbon particles released from burning fuels. □□□

Answers

1 A central nucleus with electrons arranged around it.
2 Groups.
3 They are shared or transferred between atoms.
4 The compound contains one hydrogen, one nitrogen and three oxygen atoms.
5 Calcium carbonate $CaCO_3$.
6 copper carbonate → copper oxide + carbon dioxide

7 Any two from: buildings, roads, glass, iron, cement, mortar, concrete, neutralising acidity in soil or lakes.
8 Iron from the blast furnace is too brittle and pure iron is too soft.
9 A mixture of a metal with other metals or non-metals.
10 The extraction of titanium needs several steps, each of which needs a lot of energy. The extraction of aluminium needs electricity, which is expensive.

11 A compound of hydrogen and carbon only.
12 The oil is heated to evaporate the hydrocarbons. The vapours rise up a column which is hotter at the bottom. They condense at different levels according to their boiling points.
13 Water vapour and carbon dioxide.
14 One from: global dimming, blackens buildings, makes it difficult to breathe.

Alkenes

1 Why are alkenes described as unsaturated? ☐ ☐ ☐

2 Give the formula for butene, which contains four carbon atoms. ☐ ☐ ☐

3 Outline how alkenes are produced from crude oil fractions. ☐ ☐ ☐

4 Describe what you would see if bromine water were shaken with ethane and ethene. ☐ ☐ ☐

Polymers

5 Name the polymer formed by the polymerisation of ethene. ☐ ☐ ☐

6 Explain why plastics are difficult to dispose of once used. ☐ ☐ ☐

7 What does a plasticiser do? ☐ ☐ ☐

Plant oils and food additives

8 What is an emulsion and how are they used in food? ☐ ☐ ☐

9 Outline how vegetable oils are hardened. ☐ ☐ ☐

10 Describe a problem caused by some food additives. ☐ ☐ ☐

Earth and atmosphere

11 Name the three main layers of the Earth, in order, starting from the centre of the Earth. ☐ ☐ ☐

12 What happens where tectonic plates meet? ☐ ☐ ☐

13 Name the two main gases in the atmosphere and their approximate proportions. ☐ ☐ ☐

14 Outline three reasons why the amount of carbon dioxide in the atmosphere decreased over millions of years. ☐ ☐ ☐

Answers

1 They contain a carbon–carbon double bond.

2 C_4H_8 (*not* C^4H^8).

3 Fractions are heated strongly and their vapours are passed over a hot catalyst. This breaks the longer alkanes into shorter alkanes and alkenes.

4 No change with ethane (bromine water stays brown) but the bromine water is decolourised in ethene.

5 Poly(ethene).

6 Many are not biodegradable so they do not rot away easily.

7 It allows the polymer molecules to slide over each more easily, making the polymer soft and flexible.

8 A mixture of an oil and water. They are used in foods such as ice cream and salad dressing. They improve the texture and appearance of food.

9 They are heated with hydrogen to about 60 °C in the presence of a nickel catalyst.

10 Some people are allergic to some food additives.

11 Core, mantle, crust.

12 Earthquakes and volcanic eruptions.

13 4/5 nitrogen and 1/5 oxygen (allow 78% or 80% nitrogen, and 21% or 20% oxygen).

14 Three from: carbon dioxide dissolved in the oceans; plants absorbed it because of photosynthesis; it became locked away as fossil fuels; it became locked away in carbonate rocks.

Physics Unit P1a   Energy and Electricity

Heat transfer and efficiency

1 Which methods of heat transfer need particles? ☐ ☐ ☐

2 Why are buildings in hot countries often painted white? ☐ ☐ ☐

3 What is 'wasted' energy? ☐ ☐ ☐

4 A coal-fired power station produces 35 MJ from 100 MJ of chemical energy stored in coal. What is its efficiency? ☐ ☐ ☐

5 A 500 W microwave oven is switched on for 12 minutes. How many units of electricity does it use? ☐ ☐ ☐

6 If a unit of electricity costs 10p, how much does it cost to run a 2 kW electric fire for 3 hours? ☐ ☐ ☐

The National Grid

7 What is the National Grid? ☐ ☐ ☐

8 A transformer changes the voltage of an electricity supply from 230 V to 25 000 V. What sort of transformer is it? ☐ ☐ ☐

9 Why is electricity sent through overhead cables at high voltages? ☐ ☐ ☐

10 What is the voltage of the domestic electricity supply? ☐ ☐ ☐

Generating electricity

11 Name two nuclear fuels and three fossil fuels. ☐ ☐ ☐

12 What is the thermal energy released from fuels used for in a power station? ☐ ☐ ☐

13 State one advantage and one disadvantage of a wind turbine. ☐ ☐ ☐

14 State one advantage and one disadvantage of a coal-fired power station. ☐ ☐ ☐

Answers

1 Conduction and convection.

2 Light surfaces are poor absorbers of infra red radiation so the buildings stay cool in the sunshine.

3 Energy that is not usefully transferred.

4 $35 \div 100 = 0.35$

5 $(500 \div 1000) \times (12 \div 60) = 0.1$ kWh

6 $2 \times 3 \times 10 = 60$p

7 The network of transmission cables and transformers that distribute electricity from power stations to consumers.

8 A step-up transformer.

9 It reduces energy losses as heat from the cables (as the current will be lower than at low voltages).

10 230 V

11 Nuclear fuels: uranium, plutonium. Fossil fuels: coal, oil and natural gas.

12 It boils water and the steam drives a turbine, which turns a generator.

13 Advantages: renewable energy source, no pollution. Disadvantages: only work when it is windy enough, spoils the view.

14 Advantages: reliable, cheap fuel. Disadvantages: non-renewable fuel used, produces harmful gases (e.g. carbon dioxide, a greenhouse gas).

Waves and electromagnetic radiation

1 What is the equation that links the wave speed, frequency and wavelength of a wave? ☐ ☐ ☐

2 Calculate the speed of a wave which has a frequency of 3400 Hz and a wavelength of 0.1 m. ☐ ☐ ☐

3 How do you know that the wave described in question 2 is unlikely to be an electromagnetic wave? ☐ ☐ ☐

4 Put these types of electromagnetic radiation into order of decreasing frequency (increasing wavelength): gamma rays, infra red rays, microwaves, radio waves, ultraviolet rays, visible light, X-rays. ☐ ☐ ☐

5 Why do hospital radiographers wear lead aprons? ☐ ☐ ☐

6 Which type of communication signal, analogue or digital, is most affected by noise? ☐ ☐ ☐

Atomic radiation

7 Name the two types of particle found in the nucleus of an atom. ☐ ☐ ☐

8 What are isotopes? ☐ ☐ ☐

9 Which types of radiation (alpha, beta or gamma) are deflected by magnetic fields? ☐ ☐ ☐

10 A radioactive source emits radiation that is stopped by lead and thin aluminium, but not by paper. What type of radiation does it emit? ☐ ☐ ☐

11 The half-life of a certain radioisotope is 20 minutes. Starting with 1 g of the isotope, how much is left after one hour? ☐ ☐ ☐

Earth and atmosphere

12 State one advantage and one disadvantage of space-based optical telescopes, compared to ground-based ones. ☐ ☐ ☐

13 Outline the Big Bang theory of the universe. ☐ ☐ ☐

14 Describe two ways in which red-shift data supports the Big Bang theory. ☐ ☐ ☐

Answers

1 wave speed = frequency × wavelength

2 wave speed = 3400 × 0.1 = 340 m/s

3 Electromagnetic radiation travels very much faster.

4 Gamma rays, X-rays, ultraviolet rays, visible light, infra red rays, microwaves, radio waves.

5 Lead absorbs radiation so it reduces the exposure to X-rays (which can be harmful).

6 Analogue.

7 Protons and neutrons.

8 Atoms with the same number of protons but different numbers of neutrons.

9 Alpha and beta.

10 Beta.

11 0.125 g (60 ÷ 20 = 3 half-lives, so 1 → 0.5 → 0.25 → 0.125)

12 Advantage: can be used all the time, are not obscured by the atmosphere or clouds. Disadvantage: expensive and difficult to maintain.

13 The universe began as a very small point that rapidly expanded billions of years ago, and continues to expand.

14 Light from galaxies is red-shifted, so the galaxies are moving away. The light from the most distant galaxies is most red-shifted, so they are moving away fastest. These are features of particles in an explosion.

Biology B1a   Human Biology

1 Complete the sentences about reflex actions. Use these words:

effectors, motor, receptors, relay, sensory

_____ detect a stimulus. _____ neurones carry signals to the spinal cord.

Here the signals are passed along _____ neurones to _____ neurones.

These neurones lead to _____, which bring about a response.

2 Tick the correct boxes to show how different substances leave the body.

substance	lungs	skin	kidneys
water			
ions			
carbon dioxide			

3 Use straight lines to match the words and phrases. One has been done for you.

FSH ◆   ◆ secreted by the ovaries

oestrogen ◆   ◆ causes an egg to be released

LH ◆   ◆ causes an egg to mature

oral contraceptives ◆————————————————◆ prevent FSH being produced

4 Complete the table about the immune response by ticking the true or false boxes.

	true	false
pathogens are caused by disease		
white blood cells produce antibodies		
antibiotics kill bacteria and viruses		
vaccines contain a dead or inactive form of the disease		

1 Put a tick in each box against the things that plants compete with one another for.

light ☐   food ☐   water ☐   space ☐

2 Complete the sentences about reproduction. Use these words:

asexual, clones, eggs, gametes, sexual, sperm, variety

Sex cells are called _____. Male sex cells are called _____ and female sex cells are called _____.

Reproduction involving two parents is called _____ reproduction and leads to _____ in the offspring.

Reproduction involving one parent is called _____ reproduction and leads to _____.

3 Use straight lines to match the words and phrases about cloning. One has been done for you.

tissue culture   ◆   ◆   nucleus taken out of a host egg cell
embryo transplant   ◆   ◆   separated cells are implanted into host mothers
fusion cell cloning   ◆   ◆   used to clone plants
adult cell cloning   ◆━━━━━━━━━◆   donor nucleus comes from an adult cell

4 Complete the table about evolution. Put a tick against each sentence to say whether it is part of Lamarck's theory or Darwin's theory.

	Lamarck	Darwin
characteristics improved through use are inherited by offspring		
individuals in a species show variation		
individuals most suited to their environment are more likely to survive to reproduce		
characteristics that are not used disappear		

5 a) Name two greenhouse gases.

1 _____   2 _____

b) What does a greenhouse gas do?

_____

Chemistry C1a   Products from Rocks

1 Balance these equations:

a) $Mg + \underline{\quad} HCl \rightarrow MgCl_2 + H_2$

b) $\underline{\quad} Cu + O_2 \rightarrow \underline{\quad} CuO$

c) $\underline{\quad} Fe + \underline{\quad} O_2 \rightarrow \underline{\quad} Fe_2O_3$

2 Use straight lines to match the words and phrases about limestone and its products.

limestone ◆	◆ $Ca(OH)_2$ ◆	◆ calcium carbonate
quicklime ◆	◆ CaO ◆	◆ calcium hydroxide
slaked lime ◆	◆ $CaCO_3$ ◆	◆ calcium oxide

3 Which part of the periodic table contains the transition metals?

Part containing transition metals:

_____

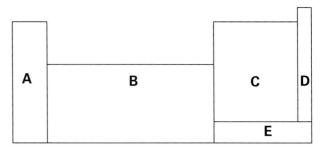

4 Complete the following table about alkanes.

alkane	molecular formula	structural formula
methane	CH_4	
ethane		H H | | H—C—C—H | | H H
propane	C_3H_8	

5 Complete the word equation about hydrocarbon fuels burning:

a) hydrocarbon + _____ → _____ + carbon dioxide

b) What problem does sulfur dioxide from burning fuels cause?

Problem: _____

1 Complete the table about hydrocarbons.

Put a tick against each statement to say whether it is about alkanes or about alkenes.

	alkanes	alkenes
general formula C_nH_{2n}		
general formula C_nH_{2n+2}		
decolourise bromine water		
useful as monomers		
have double bonds		
have single bonds		
saturated		

2 Complete the sentences about plant oils and food additives. Use these words:

chromatography, emulsions, fats, hardened, hydrogen, unsaturated

_____ vegetable oils contain carbon–carbon double bonds. They can be _____ by reacting

them with _____. These _____ are useful for making cakes, margarines and pastry.

Oil and water mix together to make _____. Artificial colours can be analysed by _____.

3 a) Starting with the atmosphere and working towards the centre of the Earth, name the Earth's three main layers in order.

atmosphere → _____ → _____ → _____

b) What makes tectonic plates move?

_____

4 Complete the following table about the evolution of the Earth's atmosphere.

gas	change over time	reason for change
carbon dioxide		1 dissolved in oceans 2 3 4
oxygen		
water vapour	decreased	
ammonia and methane		reaction with oxygen

Physics P1a   Energy and Electricity

1 Complete the following table about the transfer of thermal energy.

method of transfer	needs particles	example
conduction		
convection	yes	
		heat from the Sun reaching the Earth

2 Put a tick against the most efficient and the least efficient device in the list.

	most efficient	least efficient
250 J supplied, 100 J usefully transferred		
4 MJ supplied, 3 MJ usefully transferred		
250 J supplied, 50 J wasted		
10 J supplied, 3 J wasted		

3 Complete the sentences about the National Grid. Use these words:

high, increases, low, reduces, step-down, step-up

The National Grid transfers electricity from power stations to consumers.

A _____ transformer _____ the voltage from the power station to the transmission lines.

The _____ voltage _____ energy losses during transmission. A _____ transformer

reduces the voltage to make it _____ enough for the domestic electricity supply.

4 Use straight lines to match the words and phrases about generating electricity from different energy sources.

renewable
energy source   ◆

◆   gas   ◆   ◆   only works during the day
◆   solar power   ◆   ◆   produces a lot of carbon dioxide
◆   nuclear power   ◆   ◆   may harm wading birds
◆   tidal power   ◆   ◆   good for base load electricity

1 a) Complete the following table about the electromagnetic spectrum.
Delete high or low and long or short as appropriate.

type of radiation		X–rays		infra red		radio waves
typical use	sterilising surgical equipment		sun beds		cooking and com-munication	
frequency	high/low					low/high
wavelength	long/short					short/long

b) Which type of electromagnetic radiation is missing from the table?

Type of radiation: _____

c) Where should it go?

Between _____ and _____

d) Which type of signal is least affected by noise, analogue or digital?

Type of signal: _____

2 Put a tick against the correct properties of the different types of radiation.

	alpha	beta	gamma
stopped by paper			
stopped by aluminium sheet			
stopped by lead			
made of particles			
deflected by magnetic fields			

3 Complete the sentences by selecting the correct word from each pair.

The Big Bang theory states that the **galaxy/universe** began as a **tiny/huge** single point.

Light from **distant/nearby** galaxies is more red-shifted than light from **distant/nearby** galaxies,

so galaxies are moving **towards/away from** us.

Biology B1a

Nervous system (p9)

1 It is the junction between two nerve cells.
2 hot object (stimulus) → receptor in skin → signal travels through a sensory neurone → signal travels through a relay neurone → signal travels through a motor neurone → muscle (effector) moves hand away.

Hormones (p11)

1 Two from: water content, ion content, blood sugar level, temperature.
2 Through the bloodstream.
3 Allows both fast and slow responses and effects that are short-lived or long-lasting.

Controlling reproduction (p13)

1 Pituitary gland. It causes eggs to mature and stimulates the ovaries to produce oestrogen.
2 Ovaries. It stimulates the pituitary gland to make LH and inhibits production of FSH.
3 FSH increases the woman's natural level of FSH and makes it more likely that eggs will mature. Oestrogen inhibits FSH production and can be used as an oral contraceptive.

Diet and exercise (p15)

1 A diet containing the correct nutrients in the right amounts, which supplies the right amount of energy.
2 Problems such as: becoming too thin, periods in women stopping, reduced resistance to infection, named deficiency disease such as rickets from lack of vitamin D.
3 Problems such as: becoming too fat, heart disease, high blood pressure, diabetes, arthritis.

Cholesterol and salt (p17)

1 The liver.
2 LDLs are 'bad' cholesterol and HDLs are 'good' cholesterol. LDLs take cholesterol from the liver to the cells and HDLs take cholesterol from the cells to the liver.
3 Processed foods often contain a lot of fat, which can increase body weight and cholesterol levels, leading to cardiovascular disease. Processed foods often contain a lot of salt, which causes high blood pressure in 30% of the population.

Medical drugs (p19)

1 A substance that affects the body.
2 Laboratory testing with computer models and cells, then animal testing to look for side-effects, then testing in human volunteers.
3 Thalidomide causes birth defects, so it cannot be prescribed if there is any chance of a woman being pregnant, or becoming pregnant, while they are taking it.

Recreational drugs (p21)

1 To become dependent on something and find it difficult to give up.
2 Nicotine is the addictive substance, carbon monoxide reduces the oxygen-carrying capacity of the blood, tar causes cancer.
3 Nerves and brain, and, in the longer term, the liver.
4 Smokers are addicted and will suffer unpleasant withdrawal symptoms if they try to give up. Social pressure from friends and family may make it difficult or undesirable to stop.

Pathogens and disease (p23)

1 A microorganism that can cause infectious disease.

2 They reproduce rapidly inside the body and release toxins.
3 They ingest pathogens, they produce antitoxins, they produce antibodies that destroy particular pathogens.

Antibiotics (p25)

1 A substance that can kill bacteria.
2 Colds are caused by viruses, not bacteria, and antibiotics only work against bacteria.
3 Antibiotic-resistant strains could appear if antibiotics are over-used.

Vaccination (p27)

1 Small amounts of dead or inactive pathogens.
2 It causes the production of white blood cells that can produce antibodies against it. Some of these remain after the vaccine has been destroyed. If the pathogen infects the body, these white blood cells reproduce rapidly and produce a lot of antibodies very quickly.
3 Flu viruses mutate so one year's vaccine may not protect against the following year's strains of flu viruses.

Biology B1b

Adaptation (p29)

1 Three from: food, water, mates, territory.
2 The tree competes with the grass for light, water and nutrients.
3 Camouflage against the snow in winter and the ground in summer.

Reproduction (p31)

1 In the nucleus.
2 The offspring get half their genetic information from one parent and half from the other, so the genetic information is mixed.

3 There is only one parent and no mixing of genetic information.

Cloning and genetic engineering (p33)

1 Taking cuttings and letting them grow. Tissue culture of small groups of cells.
2 The host mother provides the womb for the embryo to grow in, but not its genetic information. The genetic information comes from the original embryo.
3 Use adult cell cloning: take the nucleus out of an egg cell, replace it with the nucleus from one of the horse's body cells, implant the egg into a host mother.

Extinction and evolution (p35)

1 The remains of a prehistoric animal or plant, preserved in the Earth's crust.
2 The rats might eat their eggs, or compete for food.
3 Simple life form developed on the Earth more than three billion years ago and all species of living things evolved from these.

Natural selection (p37)

1 Individuals in a species are not all the same. This is because of their genes. Individuals most suited to their environment survive to reproduce. Their offspring inherit the genes that made them successful.
2 It conflicted with religious views; people could not understand how complex features could evolve.
3 Bacteria are suited to their environment. They will continue to exist unless they cannot adapt to changes in their environment.

Pollution (p39)

1 The population and standard of living are increasing.
2 Chemicals such as fertilisers, herbicides and pesticides can be washed into rivers and lakes.

3 The air in towns is likely to be more polluted than the air in the countryside, so fewer lichens grow there.
4 Metal ores are a non-renewable resource, so they will run out one day. If we recycle metals, it will increase the time taken for metal ores to run out. They may not run out at all.

Global warming (p41)

1 A gas that is particularly good at absorbing and emitting thermal energy in the atmosphere.
2 Any one of: rise in sea levels, big changes in climate, melting ice caps.
3 Rice paddy fields and cattle release methane. Clearing forests for farming reduces the number of trees available to absorb carbon dioxide. Decay microorganisms and burning the trees release carbon dioxide.

Chemistry C1a

Atoms and elements (p43)

1 Central nucleus surrounded by electrons.
2 A substance made from only one sort of atom.
3 A column containing elements with similar properties.

Reactions and compounds (p45)

1 $6 + 16 = 22 g$
2 Each molecule contains six atoms of carbon, twelve atoms of hydrogen, and six atoms of oxygen.
3 They are moved from one atom to another, or shared between two atoms.
4 $C + 2CuO \rightarrow CO_2 + 2Cu$

Limestone (p47)

1 Advantages: local employment, produces useful raw material. Disadvantages: noisy, dusty, may reduce tourist trade, leaves a big hole.

2 Large building projects need lots of concrete, steel (from iron), glass and new roads. Limestone is a raw material for producing these materials.

Ores and iron (p49)

1 A rock or mineral that contains enough metal to make it worthwhile extracting the metal.
2 Lead is less reactive than carbon but aluminium is more reactive than carbon.
3 It is 96% iron. The impurities it contains makes it hard but brittle.

Alloys (p51)

1 A mixture of a metal with non-metals or other metals.
2 In a pure metal the layers of atoms can slide over each other easily. In an alloy, the different-sized atoms distort the regular arrangement of atoms so that the layers do not slide over each other easily.
3 High carbon steel is hard. It would be difficult to press it into shape.

Copper, titanium and aluminium (p53)

1 It does not react with water and it is easily bent into shape.
2 A lot of energy is needed to extract them. Titanium is extracted in several steps. Aluminium is extracted using electricity.
3 Just one step should reduce the cost of extracting titanium. If titanium is cheaper, it should be used more widely.

Hydrocarbons (p55)

1 A compound of hydrogen and carbon only.
2 C_6H_{14}
3 The crude oil is heated to evaporate it, then allowed to condense at different temperatures.
4 The fractions at the top contain shorter alkanes, which are runnier and easier to light.

Burning fuels (p57)

1 Four from: water vapour, carbon dioxide, carbon monoxide, particles, sulfur dioxide.
2 Complete combustion happens when there is plenty of air. Incomplete combustion happens when there is not enough air. Carbon monoxide is produced instead of carbon dioxide in incomplete combustion.
3 Fewer particles will cause global dimming to decrease. More sunlight will reach the Earth's surface, increasing the amount of thermal energy that could be trapped by the atmosphere.

Chemistry C1b

Alkenes (p59)

1 Cracking is the breakdown of long alkanes to form shorter alkanes and alkenes. The alkanes are vaporised and passed over a hot catalyst. This is done because the demand for shorter alkanes cannot be met by fractional distillation alone.
2 C_6H_{12}
3 The ethene would come from crude oil and that would not sound very appealing.

Polymers (p61)

1 Poly(chloroethene).
2 HDPE would be better. HDPE is stronger than LDPE. Hot drinks would be too hot for LDPE but not for HDPE, which is useable up to 120°C.
3 Alkenes used as monomers are obtained by cracking crude oil fractions. If the cost of oil goes up, so will the cost of polymers.

Plant oils (p63)

1 Crush the plant material. Press to remove the oil, or dissolve the oil in solvent then distil to remove the solvent.
2 They are a source of energy and nutrients such as vitamins.
3 A mixture of oil and water. Found in ice cream, salad dressings.
4 React with hydrogen at about 60°C in the presence of a nickel catalyst. Hardened vegetable oils are solid at room temperature and can be used in margarine, and for making cakes and pastries.

Food additives (p65)

1 Two from: improve taste, improve appearance, improve shelf life.
2 The additives are listed on the ingredients label.
3 Banned food additives may get into food by mistake, some people have allergies to certain additives.

Structure of the Earth (p67)

1 It has a layered structure. The innermost layer is a core made from iron and nickel. The next layer is the mantle, made from rock that can flow very slowly. The outermost layer is a rocky crust.
2 Mountains should be all over the surface and they are not.
3 The coasts of South America and Africa fit together; similar rocks are found on both continents; similar fossils are found on both continents.
4 Boundaries between tectonic plates.

The atmosphere (p69)

1 Carbon dioxide.
2 Nitrogen.
3 Carbon dioxide: dissolved in oceans, formed fossil fuels, formed carbonate rocks.
   Oxygen: produced by plants because of photosynthesis.
4 These events happened a very long time ago. No-one was there to see them and record observations, so the theories must be based on evidence left behind.

Noble gases (p71)

1 Three from: helium, neon, argon, krypton, xenon, radon.
2 It is much less dense than air.
3 It is unreactive, so it stops the metal filament burning away.
4 The noble gases are unreactive, so do not form compounds.

Physics P1a

Heat transfer (p73)

1 The thermal energy travels through space as infra red radiation.
2 The lid reduces heat loss by convection.
3 Shiny surfaces are poor absorbers and emitters of thermal energy. The shiny foil helps to stop the satellite or spacecraft getting too hot or too cold.

Efficiency (p75)

1 Energy that is not usefully transferred or transformed.
2 The surroundings warm up and the energy becomes spread out too thinly to be useful.
3 35 MJ
4 0.7

Cost of electricity (p77)

1 The watt, W.
2 energy transferred = power × time
3 $250 \div 1000 \times 8 = 2$ kWh
4 $100 \div 1000 \times 6 \times 10 = 6$p

The National Grid (p79)

1 The network of cables that transfers electricity from the power stations to the consumers.
2 High voltages reduce the current in the cables, which reduces energy losses from them.

3 Step-up transformers increase the voltage from the power stations for transmission in the cables. Step-down transformers reduce the voltage to safer levels for distribution to consumers.

Generating electricity (p81)

1 Fossil fuels: oil, coal, natural gas. Nuclear fuels: uranium, plutonium.
2 Thermal energy released from the fuel is used to boil water. The steam drives a turbine. This is connected to a generator, which turns and produces electricity.
3 There are several energy transfer and transformation steps, and each of these will produce waste energy.

Renewable energy sources (p83)

1 Wave machines use the rise and fall of water because of waves. Tidal barrages use the kinetic energy in moving water as the tide changes. Hydroelectric power schemes use the kinetic energy from water stored in dams to turn electricity generators.
2 Satellites are too high up to run cables to them. There is no night or cloud in space, and the cells should supply electricity constantly unless the satellite goes into the Earth's shadow.
3 If the thermal energy is extracted too quickly, the rocks will become too cold to be useful.

Resources compared (p85)

1 They can be started up quickly but their fuel is expensive.
2 They take a long time to start up but their fuel is cheap.
3 The advantages of each type of power station can be exploited and their disadvantages overcome.

Physics P1b

The electromagnetic spectrum (p87)

1 wave speed = frequency × wavelength
2 wave speed = 2 400 000 000 × 0.125 = 300 000 000 m/s
3 Ultraviolet

Some uses of electromagnetic radiation (p89)

1 We feel it as heat.
2 Water, fats and sugars in food easily absorb microwaves. The molecules vibrate more vigorously and the food heats up.
3 The X-rays pass through the metal parts allowing a picture to be taken without taking the machinery apart.

Communication signals (p91)

1 Analogue signals are continuously varying but digital signals have certain states, usually 0 and 1. Digital signals are affected less by noise.
2 The light is repeatedly reflected inside the fibre.
3 Microwaves pass through the atmosphere.

Hazards of electromagnetic radiation (p93)

1 X-rays are absorbed by lead.
2 The clothing absorbs ultraviolet light and reduces exposure to it.
3 Metal mesh in the door to stop microwave radiation escaping and safety lock so the oven does not work with an open door.

Atomic radiation (p95)

1 Atoms that have the same number of protons but different numbers of neutrons.

2 Alpha radiation and beta radiation.
3 Two from: alpha is stopped by paper but beta and gamma are not; alpha and beta are stopped by thin aluminium but gamma is not; gamma travels further in air than alpha and beta; alpha is the most ionising and gamma is the least ionising.

Half-life (p97)

1 One from: the time taken for half the nuclei of that isotope in a sample to decay; or the time taken for the count rate from a sample to fall to half the starting rate.
2 0.5 g (240 ÷ 60 = 4 half-lives, so 8 g → 4 g → 2 g → 1 g → 0.5 g)
3 It is a gamma emitter so it passes out of the patient's body without harming them and is easily detected, and it has a short half-life so that it will not persist in the body for a long time.

Observing the universe (p99)

1 They work during the day and in bad weather; they provide more detailed images.
2 The idea that the universe began from a very small point about 13.6 billion years ago, and expanded rapidly. It continues to expand.
3 The light from galaxies is red-shifted, showing that the galaxies are moving away from us. The more distant the galaxy, the more its light is red-shifted. This shows that more distant galaxies are moving more quickly. These features are shared by explosions, where the fastest objects travel furthest.

Biology B1a

1 receptors, sensory, relay, motor, effectors

2

substance	lungs	skin	kidneys
water	✔	✔	✔
ions		✔	✔
carbon dioxide	✔		

3

FSH — causes an egg to mature
oestrogen — secreted by the ovaries
LH — causes an egg to be released
oral contraceptives — prevent FSH being produced

4

	true	false
pathogens are caused by disease		✔
white blood cells produce antibodies	✔	
antibiotics kill bacteria and viruses		✔
vaccines contain a dead or inactive form of the disease		✔

Biology B1b

1 light, water and space

2 gametes, sperm, eggs, sexual, variety, asexual, clones

3

tissue culture — used to clone plants
embryo transplant — separated cells are implanted into host mothers
fusion cell cloning — nucleus taken out of a host egg cell
adult cell cloning — donor nucleus comes from an adult cell

4

	Lamarck	Darwin
characteristics improved through use are inherited by offspring	✔	
individuals in a species show variation		✔
individuals most suited to their environment are more likely to survive to reproduce		✔
characteristics that are not used disappear	✔	

5 a) Methane, carbon dioxide
b) Absorbs thermal energy in the atmosphere and radiates it back to the Earth, keeping the planet warmer than it would be without the greenhouse gas.

Chemistry C1a

1 a) $Mg + 2HCl \rightarrow MgCl_2 + H_2$
b) $2Cu + O_2 \rightarrow 2CuO$
c) $4Fe + 3O_2 \rightarrow 2Fe_2O_3$

2

limestone — CaCO₃
quicklime — CaO
slaked lime — Ca(OH)₂
→ calcium carbonate, calcium hydroxide, calcium oxide

3 Part B

4

alkane	molecular formula	structural formula
methane	CH_4	H–C–H with H above and below
ethane	C_2H_6	
propane	C_3H_8	

5 a) hydrocarbon + **oxygen** → **water** + carbon dioxide
b) Acid rain

Chemistry C1b

1

	alkanes	alkenes
general formula C_nH_{2n}		✔
general formula C_nH_{2n+2}	✔	
decolourise bromine water		✔
useful as monomers		✔
have double bonds		✔
have single bonds	✔	✔
saturated	✔	

2 unsaturated, hardened, hydrogen, fats, emulsions, chromatography

3 a) atmosphere → crust → mantle → core
b) Convection currents in the mantle driven by heat produced from natural radioactive processes inside the Earth.

4

gas	change over time	reason for change
carbon dioxide	decreased	1 dissolved in oceans
		2 photosynthesis by plants
		3 locked up in fossil fuels
		4 locked up in carbonate rocks
oxygen	increased	photosynthesis by plants
water vapour	decreased	condensed to form the oceans
ammonia and methane	decreased	reaction with oxygen

Physics P1a

1

method of transfer	needs particles	example
conduction	yes	e.g. heat passing through a metal pan
convection	yes	e.g. hot air from a radiator filling a room
radiation	no	heat from the Sun reaching the Earth

2

	most efficient	least efficient
250 J supplied, 100 J usefully transferred		✔
4 MJ supplied, 3 MJ usefully transferred		
250 J supplied, 50 J wasted	✔	
10 J supplied, 3 J wasted		

3 step-up, increases, high, reduces, step-down, low

4

renewable energy source

gas
solar power
nuclear power
tidal power

only works during the day
produces a lot of carbon dioxide
may harm wading birds
good for base load electricity

Physics P1b

1 a)

type of radiation	gamma	X-rays	ultraviolet	infra red	microwave	radio waves
typical use	sterilising surgical equipment	medical images	sun beds	signals	cooking and com-munication	TV and radio
frequency	high/~~low~~					low/~~high~~
wavelength	~~long~~/short					~~short~~/long

b) visible light
c) between ultraviolet and infra red
d) digital

2

	alpha	beta	gamma
stopped by paper	✔		
stopped by aluminium sheet	✔	✔	
stopped by lead	✔	✔	✔
made of particles	✔	✔	
deflected by magnetic fields	✔	✔	

3 Correct words from each pair: galaxy, tiny, distant, nearby, away from

A

adaptation   Feature of an organism that makes it suited for living in its habitat.

alloy   A mixture of a metal with non-metals or other metals.

alpha radiation   Atomic radiation consisting of alpha particles, two protons and two neutrons joined together.

amplitude   The distance between the maximum disturbance of a wave and its undisturbed position.

analogue signal   Communication signal that varies continuously.

antibiotic   Chemical that can kill bacteria.

antibody   Protein produced by white blood cells, capable of attaching to particular antigens.

antigen   Substance recognised as foreign to the body.

antitoxin   Chemical produced by white blood cells that counteracts a toxin.

asexual reproduction   Producing offspring from just one parent.

atmosphere   Layer of gas surrounding the Earth.

atom   Tiny particle that all substances are made from.

B

bacterium (plural **bacteria**)   Tiny single-celled organism.

balanced diet   A diet that contains the required nutrients in the correct amounts for health.

balanced equation   Description of a chemical reaction that shows the number and formulae of each substance involved.

beta radiation   Atomic radiation consisting of beta particles, electrons from the nucleus.

Big Bang theory   The idea that the universe began as a very small point that expanded rapidly, and continues to do so.

biodegradable   Able to be broken down by microorganisms.

bond   Join or force of attraction between two atoms.

C

catalyst   A substance that speeds up chemical reactions without being used up itself.

chemical bond   See *bond*.

chemical formula   Combination of numbers and chemical symbols that shows how many of each sort of atom are in a compound.

chemical symbol   One, two or three letters that represent an element.

cholesterol   A substance made using saturated fats in the liver.

chromatography   Method used to detect and identify coloured substances.

chromosome   Object in the nucleus carrying genes.

clone   Genetically identical individual.

combustion   Burning – the reaction of a fuel with oxygen.

compound   Substance made from more than one element chemically joined together.

condense   To turn from a gas to liquid.

conduction   The transfer of thermal energy by passing vibrations from one particle to the next in a substance.

convection   The transfer of thermal energy in a liquid or gas by particles moving from place to place.

convection current   The circulating movement of liquids or gases caused by heating.

core   Innermost layer of the Earth, made from iron and nickel.

corrosion   The reaction of a metal with air and water, such as rusting.

cracking   Thermal decomposition reaction in which longer alkanes are broken down into shorter alkanes and alkenes.

crust   Outermost layer of the Earth, made from rock.

D

density   The mass of a piece of material divided by its volume.

digital signal   Communication signal with discrete states, 0 and 1, or ON and OFF.

drug   A substance that changes chemical processes in the body.

E

E number   Unique number given to food additives to show that they have been tested and passed as safe to use.

effector   Part of the body that responds to a stimulus, such as a muscle or gland.

efficiency   A measure of the proportion of energy supplied to a device that is usefully transferred.

electron   Particles in an atom arranged around its nucleus.

element   Substance from just one type of atom.

embryo transplant   Separating cells from an early embryo and transplanting the identical embryos into host mothers.

emulsion   Mixture of oil and water.

environment   The conditions in a habitat.

ethanol   The alcohol in alcoholic drinks, C_2H_5OH.

evaporate   To turn from a liquid to a gas.

evolution   Development of a type of living thing from an earlier, simpler life form.

extinct   When a species no longer has any living members left.

F

fertilisation   Joining or fusion of gametes.

food additive   Natural or artificial substance added to food to improve its properties.

fossil fuel   Fuel formed from the ancient remains of dead plants or animals.

fractional distillation   Method used to separate mixtures which relies on the different substances having different boiling points.

fractionating column   The equipment used to separate crude oil by fractional distillation.

fractions The individual parts separated by fractional distillation.

frequency The number of waves that pass a certain point each second, measured in hertz, Hz.

FSH Hormone secreted by the pituitary gland which causes eggs to mature.

G

gametes Sex cells. Sperm are male sex cells and eggs are female sex cells.

gamma radiation Part of the electromagnetic spectrum, used for sterilising surgical instruments.

gene Section of DNA in a chromosome that controls a characteristic in the body.

generator Machine that transforms kinetic energy into electrical energy.

genetic engineering Transferring genes from one cell to another.

genetic modification Another name for genetic engineering, shortened to GM.

geothermal energy Thermal energy from hot rocks deep underground.

gland Tissue or organ able to produce hormones.

global dimming Reduction in sunlight reaching the Earth's surface because of particles produced by burning fuels.

global warming Worldwide increase in average temperatures.

greenhouse effect Absorption of thermal energy in the atmosphere.

greenhouse gas Atmospheric gas that is particularly good at absorbing and emitting thermal energy.

group Column of elements in the periodic table that have similar properties.

group 0 The noble gases, found in the far right hand column of the periodic table.

H

habitat The place where an organism lives.

half-life The time taken for half the nuclei of the isotope in a sample to decay; or the time taken for the count rate from a sample to fall to half the starting rate.

hardened Vegetable oil reacted with hydrogen.

HDL High-density lipoprotein, also known as 'good' cholesterol.

hormone Chemical produced by a gland and transported in the bloodstream to a target organ.

hydrocarbons Compounds containing hydrogen and carbon only.

hydroelectric power scheme A scheme to generate electricity from water held behind a dam.

I

immune Protected against a particular infective pathogen and the disease it causes.

infra red radiation Thermal radiation, also called infra red light. It is part of the electromagnetic spectrum and is used for TV remote controls.

insulator A poor conductor of thermal energy.

ion Charged particle made when an atom loses (or gains) an electron.

ionising radiation Radiation that produces charged particles from atoms.

isotopes Atoms with the same number of protons but different numbers of neutrons.

IVF *In vitro* fertilisation – fertilising an egg outside the body in a laboratory.

J

joule The unit of energy, symbol J.

K

kilowatt-hour kWh, the unit of electrical energy transferred from the mains supply.

L

LDL Low-density lipoprotein, also known as 'bad' cholesterol.

limestone A rock made from calcium carbonate, $CaCO_3$.

lipoprotein A combination of cholesterol and protein found in the blood.

M

mantle Layer of the Earth between the crust and core, made from rock that can flow very slowly.

menstrual cycle Monthly series of changes in the reproductive system of women.

metabolic rate The speed at which the chemical reactions in the body's cells happen.

microwaves Part of the electromagnetic spectrum, used for communications and cooking food.

molecular formula Formula showing the number of atoms of each element in a compound.

monomers Small molecules that can join together to make longer molecules.

motor neurone Nerve cell that carries information to an effector.

N

National Grid The network of cables that transfers electricity from power stations to consumers.

natural selection The theory of how species change over time.

neurone Nerve cell.

neutron Neutral particle in the nucleus.

nicotine The addictive substance in tobacco smoke.

nuclear fission Change to an atom in which its nucleus breaks apart.

nuclear reaction Change to the nucleus of an atom.

nucleus The part at the centre of the atom.

O

oestrogen Hormone secreted by the ovaries which inhibits production of FSH.

optical fibre Thin rod of glass that can carry infra red and visible light signals.

ore A rock or mineral that contains enough metal to make it worthwhile extracting the metal.

P

pathogen   Microorganism that causes infectious disease.

periodic table   Chart showing the elements.

pollutant   Substance produced that harms the environment.

pollution   Waste products that harm the environment when released.

polymer   A large molecule formed from many monomers by polymerisation.

power   The rate of energy transfer.

product   A substance that is made in a chemical reaction.

proton   Positively charged particle in the nucleus.

Q

quicklime   Calcium oxide, CaO.

R

radiation   invisible particles or rays given off by nuclei of atoms.

radio waves   Part of the electromagnetic spectrum, used for transmitting television and radio programmes.

radioactive   Able to give off radiation.

reactant   A substance that reacts in a chemical reaction.

receptor   Group of cells that detects a stimulus.

red–shift   The observed light from distant galaxies is moved towards the red end of the spectrum.

reduction   Reaction in which oxygen is removed from a substance.

relay neurone   Nerve cell that passes information from a sensory neurone to a motor neurone.

renewable energy source   A source of energy that will not run out provided it is managed effectively.

renewable resources   Substances that will not run out.

S

saturated   Contains only single bonds.

sensory neurone   Nerve cell that carries information from a receptor.

sexual reproduction   Producing offspring from two parents.

slaked lime   Calcium hydroxide, $Ca(OH)_2$.

smart alloy   Mixture of metals that can return to its original shape after being bent.

solar cell   A device that converts light energy directly into electrical energy.

stimulus   Change in the surroundings detected by a receptor.

structural formula   Diagram showing how the atoms in a compound are joined together.

sustainable development   Living in such a way that we meet our needs without damaging the ability of future generations to meet their own needs.

synapse   Junction between two nerve cells.

T

tectonic plate   Piece of the crust and upper mantle.

theory of continental drift   The idea that tectonic plates move, carrying continents with them.

thermal decomposition   The chemical reaction where a compound breaks down into simpler substances when heated.

thermal energy   Heat energy.

tidal barrage   A barrier built across a river mouth to take advantage of moving water produced by the tides.

tobacco   Dried leaves from the tobacco plant, used in cigarettes.

toxin   Poison.

tracer   Radioactive substance used to follow chemicals in the environment or in the body.

transformer   A device that changes the voltage of an electrical supply.

turbine   Machine with many blades. It spins when steam is passed into it.

U

ultraviolet radiation   Part of the electromagnetic spectrum, used for sun beds.

unsaturated   Containing a carbon–carbon double bond.

V

vaccination   The process of providing a vaccine to make someone immune to a particular pathogen.

vaccine   A small amount of dead or inactive pathogens, usually injected into the body.

virus   Tiny particle of genetic information surrounded by a protein coat.

viscosity   A measure of how runny a liquid is – water has a low viscosity and treacle has a high viscosity.

volatile   Liquids that easily turn into gases are very volatile.

W

watt   The unit of power, symbol W.

wave machine   Device that converts the kinetic energy in waves into electrical energy.

wavelength   The distance between a point on one wave and the same point on the next wave, measured in metres, m.

white blood cell   A type of cell found in the blood, and which helps to defend the body against pathogens.

wind turbine   Type of windmill that generates electricity using the kinetic energy in wind.

X

X–rays   Part of the electromagnetic spectrum, used for making medical images of broken bones.

Biology Unit B1a   Human Biology

Controlling body processes

- Nerve cells are neurones. The gap between two neurones is a synapse. Chemicals diffuse across the gap so that signals can pass from one neurone to another.
- Reflex actions are fast and automatic.

part of the nervous system	what it does
receptor cell, e.g. in the skin	detects a stimulus, such as a change in temperature
sensory neurone	carries information from a receptor
relay neurone in spinal cord	carries information from a sensory neurone to a motor neurone
motor neurone	carries information to an effector
effector, e.g. a muscle or gland	carries out a response, such as a muscle moving or a gland producing a hormone

- Internal conditions in the body must be controlled, including water and ion content, blood sugar level and temperature.
- Water and ions leave the body from the skin and kidneys. Water also leaves the body from the lungs.
- Hormones are chemicals produced by glands. They are transported in the bloodstream to their target organs, where they cause a change.
- Hormones control the menstrual cycle in women, which lasts for about 28 days.

hormone	produced by	what it does
FSH	pituitary gland	causes an egg to mature stimulates oestrogen release
oestrogen	ovaries	stops FSH production simulates LH release causes the womb lining to thicken
LH	pituitary gland	causes the release of an egg at about day 14

- Oral contraceptives contain hormones that stop production of FSH, so eggs do not mature.
- Fertility drugs boost the levels of FSH. This helps more eggs mature for use in *in vitro* fertilisation or IVF.

Diet and health

- People become too thin if they do not eat enough. They become fat if they eat too much or take too little exercise.
- Lack of food can cause health problems, including irregular periods in women and reduced resistance to infection.

- The metabolic rate is the speed of chemical reactions in the body. Active people with a lot of muscle and little fat have high metabolic rates. Exercise and inherited factors also influence it.
- Heart disease, high blood pressure, arthritis and diabetes are linked to excess weight.
- Cholesterol is made by the liver from saturated fats.
- Low-density lipoproteins or LDLs are 'bad' cholesterol. They carry cholesterol from the liver to the body's cells.
- High-density lipoproteins or HDLs are 'good' cholesterol. They carry cholesterol from the body's cells to the liver.
- Processed foods often contain a lot of fat and salt. Too much salt causes high blood pressure, leading to cardiovascular disease.

Drugs

- Drugs change chemical processes inside the body. Many drugs are found naturally. New drugs are tested to make sure they are effective and safe.
- Thalidomide caused birth defects during the early 1960s. It is now used to treat leprosy, but cannot be given to pregnant women.
- Alcohol slows down reactions and leads to a loss of self-control. It can damage the liver and brain.

substance in tobacco smoke	effect on body
nicotine	addictive
carbon monoxide	reduces the ability of the blood to carry oxygen
tar	causes cancer

Pathogens and disease

- Pathogens are micro-organisms, such as bacteria and viruses, that cause disease.
- Bacteria multiply rapidly in the body and release toxins. Viruses multiply inside cells and damage them when they escape.
- White blood cells produce antitoxins and antibodies, and they ingest pathogens. Antibodies stick to certain antigens carried by pathogens.
- Antibiotics kill bacteria but not viruses. Over-use of antibiotics has produced resistant strains of bacteria because of natural selection.
- Vaccination involves injecting a dead or inactive form of a pathogen. White blood cells are produced that recognise the pathogen and produce antibodies against it.

Adaptation
- Plants compete with each other for light, water, nutrients and space.
- Animals compete with each other for food, water, mates and territory.
- Organisms have particular features, called adaptations, which allow them to survive in their environment.
- Extinction may be caused by changes to the environment, new competitors, new diseases and new predators.
- The fossil record provides evidence of how life on Earth has changed over millions of years.

Evolution
- The theory of evolution states that life developed on Earth more than three billion years ago, and that all species have evolved from these early life forms.
- Charles Darwin proposed the theory of evolution by natural selection. Individuals in a species show variation caused by differences in their genes. Individuals with features best suited to the environment are more likely to survive to reproduce and pass on their beneficial features.
- Darwin's theory was only gradually accepted and still causes controversy.
- Other theories of evolution have been proposed, but they have been disproved.

Reproduction
- Chromosomes are found in the cell's nucleus. They contain many genes, each of which controls the development of a characteristic in an organism.
- Asexual reproduction involves just one parent. All the offspring are identical because there is no mixing of genetic information. Genetically identical individuals are called clones.
- Sexual reproduction involves two parents. Fertilisation is when a male gamete and a female gamete fuse together. Genetic information is mixed, leading to variety in the offspring.

Cloning and genetic engineering
- Plants can be cloned by taking cuttings and by tissue culture.
- Animals can be cloned by embryo transplants. A developing embryo is split into separate cells at an early stage, grown in the laboratory and then transplanted into host mothers.
- Animals can also be cloned by removing the nucleus from an unfertilised egg and replacing it with the nucleus from a different cell. It is called fusion cell cloning if the nucleus comes from an embryo, and adult cell cloning if it comes from a body cell of an adult animal.
- Genetic engineering is also called genetic modification or GM. Genes are moved from one organism to another using enzymes.

Pollution
- The human population is increasing rapidly and the standard of living is improving. This increases the use of non-renewable energy resources and raw materials, and increases the amount of waste.
- Sustainable development involves meeting our needs without damaging the ability of future generations to meet their own needs.
- Waste causes pollution if it is not handled properly.
- The air can be polluted with gases such as sulfur dioxide, which causes acid rain.
- The land can be polluted with toxic chemicals, such as pesticides.
- Rivers, lakes and seas can be polluted with toxic factory waste, sewage, and chemicals washed off farmland.
- Lichens are plants that can be used as indicators of air pollution. Insect larvae and other invertebrates can be used as indicators of water pollution.

Global warming
- Carbon dioxide and methane are greenhouse gases. They absorb thermal energy and keep the planet warmer than it would be without them.
- Increasing levels of greenhouse gases leads to global warming. Increases of average temperatures by only a few degrees may cause a rise in sea levels and climate change.
- Extra methane is produced by cattle and rice paddy fields.
- Extra carbon dioxide is produced by burning fossil fuels. Deforestation makes the situation worse because there are fewer trees to absorb the carbon dioxide.

Atoms and elements

- Atoms have a nucleus at the centre with electrons arranged around it.
- An element is made of just one sort of atom. There are about 100 different elements, each with a unique chemical symbol.
- The periodic table is a chart showing information about the elements.
- Similar elements are found in columns of the periodic table called groups.

Reactions and compounds

- Reactants are the chemicals that react together, and products are the chemicals made.
- Chemical bonds between atoms involve sharing or transferring electrons between atoms.
- A compound is made of the atoms of two or more elements bonded together. A chemical formula shows the number and type of each atom present.
- No atoms are lost or made in a chemical reaction, so the total mass stays the same. Balanced equations describe reactions.

Limestone

- Limestone contains calcium carbonate, $CaCO_3$. It is used as a building material, and in the manufacture of glass, iron, cement and concrete.
- Calcium carbonate breaks down when heated to form calcium oxide (CaO) and carbon dioxide. This is called thermal decomposition. Other carbonates react in a similar way. Calcium oxide is also called quicklime.
- Calcium oxide reacts with water to form calcium hydroxide, $Ca(OH)_2$. This is also called slaked lime.

Ores and iron

- An ore is a rock that contains enough metal to make it economical to extract the metal.
- Unreactive metals are found as the metals themselves.
- Most metals are found as compounds. Metal oxides are reduced to extract the metal. If the metal is less reactive than carbon, it is extracted using carbon or carbon monoxide. Iron is extracted this way.
- Iron from the blast furnace is too brittle for most uses and pure iron is too soft. Iron is usually converted into steel.

Alloys

- An alloy is a mixture of a metal with other metals or non-metals. Steel is iron mixed with metals such as vanadium.
- Alloys are harder than individual metals because they have different sized atoms. This stops layers of atoms sliding over each other easily.
- Smart alloys have unusual properties. Shape memory alloys can be twisted and bent, but snap back into shape when warmed up.

Copper, titanium and aluminium

- Transition metals are the elements in the central block of the periodic table, such as iron, copper and titanium.
- Most high-grade copper ores have already been mined. Low-grade ores produce a lot of waste. Copper is purified by passing electricity through its solutions. Bacteria are also used to extract copper.
- Titanium cannot be extracted using carbon. Several steps are needed. Each one needs a lot of energy.
- Aluminium is in group 3. It is more reactive than carbon so it is extracted using electricity.

Alkanes

- Crude oil contains hydrocarbons, compounds of hydrogen and carbon only.
- Alkanes are unsaturated, which means that they only have single bonds. Their general formula is C_nH_{2n+2}. For example, ethane is C_2H_6.
- Fractional distillation separates the different alkanes in crude oil. This works because they have different boiling points.
- In fractional distillation, oil is heated to evaporate the hydrocarbons. The vapours rise up a tower, which is hotter at the bottom. Different fractions condense at different temperatures.

Burning fuels

- Hydrocarbons burn in plenty of air to form water vapour and carbon dioxide. If there is not enough air, carbon monoxide and particles of carbon are produced instead of carbon dioxide.
- Carbon dioxide is a greenhouse gas. Carbon particles cause global dimming.
- Many fuels contain sulfur. They produce sulfur dioxide when they burn, which causes acid rain.

Alkenes

- Alkenes are unsaturated hydrocarbons because they contain a carbon–carbon double bond. Their general formula is C_nH_{2n}. For example, ethene is C_2H_4.
- Alkenes decolourise brown bromine water but alkanes do not.
- Alkenes are produced by heating alkanes over a hot catalyst. This is called cracking. Cracking also produces shorter alkanes, which helps to meet the demand for fuels.

Products from alkenes

- Ethene reacts with steam at high temperatures and pressures to form ethanol. Ethanol can also be produced by fermentation of sugar.
- Alkenes can join together to make long molecules called polymers. The alkenes are called monomers when they do this.
- The properties of polymers depend on their monomers and the conditions used to join them together. Plasticisers are added to make polymers more flexible.
- Many polymers are not biodegradable. They do not rot away easily. This makes them difficult to dispose of after use.

Plant oils

- Vegetable oils are found in fruit, seeds and nuts. They are extracted by crushing plant materials and squeezing the oil out. They can also be extracted from crushed plant material using solvents.
- Vegetable oils are part of a balanced diet. They provide energy and contain certain vitamins. They are also used as fuels such as biodiesel.
- An emulsion is a mixture of oil and water. Emulsions are more viscous than oil or water. Emulsifiers are added to stop the oil and water separating. Emulsions are used in foods such as ice cream.
- Hydrogenated vegetable oils are used in margarine. Vegetable oils are hardened by reacting them with hydrogen.

Food additives

- Food additives are put in processed foods to improve the taste, appearance and shelf-life.
- Additives with an E number have been tested and passed as safe.
- Some food additives can cause allergic reactions in some people.
- Chromatography is used to detect and analyse artificial food colourings.

Structure of the Earth

- The Earth has a layered structure consisting of the core, mantle and crust.
- The upper part of the mantle and crust are broken into tectonic plates. These move at a few centimetres per year because of convection currents in the mantle, driven by heat from radioactive processes inside the Earth.
- The crust becomes unstable where tectonic plates meet. Earthquakes and volcanic eruptions happen there, but these are difficult to predict.
- At one time people thought that the Earth's surface features were caused by the crust shrinking as the Earth cooled.
- Alfred Wegener proposed the theory of continental drift. He could not explain how tectonic plates could move. It took many years for his theory to be generally accepted by scientists.

The atmosphere

- The Earth's atmosphere is about 80% nitrogen and 20% oxygen. There are small proportions of other gases such as carbon dioxide, water vapour and argon.
- Argon is a noble gas found in group 0. These gases are very unreactive. They are used in electric discharge tubes. Helium is a noble gas used in party balloons and airships.
- The Earth's atmosphere has been much the same for the last 200 million years.
- Scientists believe that the early atmosphere was mostly carbon dioxide, like the atmospheres of Mars and Venus today. When plants evolved, they absorbed carbon dioxide and released oxygen because of photosynthesis. Carbon dioxide also dissolved in the oceans, and became locked up in fossil fuels and carbonate rocks such as limestone.

Heat transfer

- Heat energy is also called thermal energy. The movement of atoms and molecules increases when they absorb thermal energy.
- Thermal energy can be transferred by conduction, convection and infra red radiation. Conduction and convection need particles, but radiation does not.
- Dark, dull surfaces are good emitters and absorbers of infra red radiation. Light, shiny surfaces are poor emitters and absorbers.
- The rate of transfer of thermal energy depends on the type of material, size of and shape of the object, and the difference in temperature.

Efficiency

- Energy is measured in joules, J. Energy cannot be created or destroyed, only transferred from place to place or transformed from one type to another.
- Energy that is not usefully transferred or transformed is 'wasted' energy.
- The efficiency of a device $= \dfrac{\text{useful energy transferred by device}}{\text{total energy supplied to device}}$.

Cost of electricity

- Power is measured in watts, W.
- Electrical energy from the mains supply is measured in kWh. 1 kWh is 1 unit of electricity.
- Electrical energy transferred (kWh) = power (kW) × time (h)
- Total cost of electricity = number of kWh × cost per kWh

The National Grid

- The National Grid transfers mains electricity from power stations to consumers.
- Thermal energy is lost from electricity cables. Electricity is transmitted at high voltages so that the current is low. The lower the current, the lower the amount of thermal energy lost.
- Step-up transformers increase the voltage from power stations so that energy losses are reduced. Step-down transformers decrease the voltage from the cables to safer levels for supply to homes.

Power stations

- Electricity is generated in power stations.
- Most electricity is generated in nuclear power stations or power stations fuelled by fossil fuels.
- Uranium and plutonium are nuclear fuels. Coal, oil and natural gas are fossil fuels. These fuels are non-renewable: they cannot be replaced once they have been used up.
- Thermal energy released from the fuel is used to boil water. The steam turns a turbine which drives an electricity generator.

Renewable energy sources

- Renewable energy sources will not run out, as long as they are managed effectively. There are no fuel costs but the machinery needed to use them can be expensive to build.
- Wind turbines use kinetic energy from the wind to drive electricity generators. They only work when the wind speed is high enough.
- Wave machines use the kinetic energy in waves to drive electricity generators. It has proved difficult to design machines that produce large amounts of electricity.
- Tidal barrages drive electricity generators using the moving water as the tides turn. Hydroelectric power schemes use moving water from behind dams to drive electricity generators.
- Solar cells convert light energy directly into electrical energy. They only work in the light. Geothermal power stations use hot water and steam produced deep inside the Earth.

Waves

- Waves move energy from one place to another.
- The wavelength of a wave is the distance between a point on one wave and the same point of the next wave.
- The frequency of a wave is the number of waves per second, measured in hertz, Hz.
- wave speed (m/s) = frequency (Hz) × wavelength (m)

The electromagnetic spectrum

- Electromagnetic radiation travels as waves. All electromagnetic radiation travels at the same speed in a vacuum, 300 000 000 m/s.
- The main types of electromagnetic radiation, in order of increasing wavelength and decreasing frequency are: gamma rays, X-rays, ultraviolet rays, visible light, infra red rays, microwaves and radio waves.
- Gamma rays are used to sterilise surgical instruments. X-rays are used to make medical images of bones. Ultraviolet rays are used in sun beds. Microwaves and radio waves are used for communications.

Communication signals

- Communication signals may be analogue or digital.
- Analogue signals vary continuously and digital signals have discrete states, usually 0 and 1.
- Digital signals are less affected by noise than analogue signals.
- Light travels through optical fibres, even when the fibre is bent.

Atomic radiation

- Atoms consist of a central nucleus surrounded by electrons. The nucleus contains protons and neutrons.
- Isotopes are atoms with the same number of protons but different numbers of neutrons.
- Radioactive substances give out radiation from the nuclei of their atoms. Radioactive isotopes are called radioisotopes.
- Alpha radiation, α, consists of alpha particles. An alpha particle contains two protons and two neutrons. It is identical to a helium nucleus.
- Beta radiation, β, consists of high-energy electrons emitted from the nucleus.
- Gamma radiation, γ, consists of electromagnetic radiation emitted from the nucleus.
- Alpha radiation is stopped by paper, beta radiation by thin aluminium sheeting, and gamma radiation by thick lead.
- Alpha radiation and beta radiation are deflected by electric and magnetic fields, but gamma radiation is not.
- The half-life of an isotope is the time taken for half of the isotope in a sample to decay, or the time taken for the count rate in a sample to fall to half the starting rate.

Observing the universe

- Telescopes observe the universe at different frequencies of electromagnetic radiation. Ground-based optical telescopes only work at night in clear skies but radio telescopes work all the time. Space telescopes also work all the time, but are expensive and difficult to maintain.
- The Big Bang theory of the universe states that the universe began as a tiny single point that rapidly enlarged. The universe is still expanding.
- The wavelength and frequency of a wave source changes if the source moves towards or away from you.
- Light from distant galaxies is red-shifted. This shows that the galaxies are moving away from us.
- The light from the most distant galaxies is the most red-shifted. This shows that the most distant galaxies are moving away fastest.
- Red-shift evidence supports the Big Bang theory.